The Modern Monologue
Women

Michael Earley is Chief Producer of Plays for BBC
Radio Drama in London. He was Chairman of the
Theatre Studies Program at Yale University and taught
acting, dramatic literature and playwriting there and at
New York University's Tisch School of the Arts, The
Julliard School's Acting Program, Smith College and
various other schools and universities in America and
Britain.

Philippa Keil is a writer, editor and translator who
trained at the Yale School of Drama. She graduated
from Sussex University where she acted, directed and
produced plays for the Frontdoor Theatre, and then
worked professionally in London at Richmond's Orange
Tree Theatre.

by the same authors

The Contemporary Monologue (Women)
The Modern Monologue (Men and Women)
The Classical Monologue (Men and Women)

The
Modern Monologue
Women

Edited with notes and commentaries by
MICHAEL EARLEY
& PHILIPPA KEIL

A Theatre Arts Book
Routledge
New York

First published in the U.S.A. 1993
by Theatre Arts Books / Roultedge
29 West 35th Street
New York, New York 10001

First published in Great Britain 1993
by Methuen Drama
an imprint of Reed Books Ltd
Michelin House, 81 Fulham Road, London SW3 6RB
and Auckland, Melbourne, Singapore and Toronto

ISBN 0-87830-046-5

A CIP catalogue record for this book
is avaliable at the British Libary

A CIP catalog record for this book
is available at the Library of Congress

Front cover: Elizabeth Taylor in *Cat on a Hot Tin Roof*
Photo: MGM / The Kobal Collection

Contents

Notes to the Actor

The Modern Monologue is a continuation of our previous collection *The Classical Monologue*. Here we start at the dawn of the modern age in 1892, presenting a survey of indispensable speeches from plays that continue to shape the course of modern theatre. The plays included in this collection also happen to be the ones that have helped to define modern acting in all its many guises.

Modern playwrights such as Brecht, Genet, Beckett, Ionesco, Pinter, Shepard, Guare, Nichols and Churchill, to name only a handful of the dramatists represented here, assume that a play and its characters are malleable and shifting; that mood swings, strangeness and sudden eruptions are key components of modern theatre's compelling attraction. We are, after all, not watching something 'real' but something liberated from reality; not a psychologically whole character but very often an extreme or fragmented one; not life itself but an 'imitation' of life. Theatre is manifestly theatrical. The actor is a partner in this enterprise. Her transformational talent makes a key statement about the very nature of modern drama. The modern play provokes the actor to respond freshly to the notion of what it means to be and to perform in front of others.

Modern acting is not just those specific principles formulated by Konstantin Stanislavski and his later followers; principles that relate primarily to realistic and psychologically truthful acting. Like modern drama in all its myriad forms modern acting is full of infinite possibilities. There are as many different styles of acting nowadays as there are actors to fill roles. The plays of this century have been a healthy mixture of realism and anti-realism. The speeches from Alan Ayckbourn's *Absent Friends* and Alfred Jarry's *Ubu* plays, for instance, make completely different demands on the performer. The best modern actors decide approaches to performances according to the unique demands of a role.

In looking at these modern monologues, begin by asking yourself how the speech works and what it demands from you. It may be realistic but also absurd, humorous and then pathetic, static yet suddenly physical. Tempos and pace might undergo a change. The language may be sparse, eloquent or sheer nonsense. The sentences could run-on or be brief and clipped. The speech may have a structure that is simple but ideas and arguments that are dense and complex. The modern monologue challenges the actor repeatedly to shift gears in performance and manoeuvre swiftly from style to style. That is why these speeches continue to be so exhilarating to perform. That is also why they are excellent for auditions and rehearsals. They display all dimensions of an actor's resources and stretch the imagination.

Each monologue's 'Introduction' sets the character and speech in context. In the 'Commentary' that follows the monologue we hunt out some of the clues that will help you to perform the speech better. Our remarks mean to provoke you to think for yourself about the lines, their content and what they are doing. You are free to disagree with our opinions and we hope, in fact, that you will supply your own interpretation of each speech.

At the end of the book a 'Play Source' directs you to published versions of the full texts from which we have selected these monologues. Few of these speeches will make complete sense to you until you have traced the monologue back to its source and read the entire play thoroughly. You must appreciate the whole play before taking on a part.

Michael Earley
Philippa Keil
London 1992

Absent Friends
(1974) Alan Ayckbourn

Act 1. The open-plan living-room of a modern executive-style house. Saturday afternoon.

Diana (30s) 'always gives the impression of being slightly fraught. She smiles occasionally but it's painful. Her sharp darting eyes don't miss much after years of suspicions both genuine and unfounded.' Paul, her husband, is a successful businessman who is regularly unfaithful to her. She arranges a tea party for Colin, an old friend, so that his pals can show their support for him following the recent death by drowning of his fiancée, Carol. However, Diana and her friends never actually met Carol and have not seen Colin himself in over three years. As Diana prepares for the party she ruminates about her husband to Evelyn, who has her baby with her and registers no apparent interest in the conversation.

DIANA. Him and his squash. It used to be tennis – now he's squash mad. Squash, squash, squash. Can't see what he sees in it. All afternoon hitting a ball against a wall. It's so noisy. Bang, bang, bang. He's not even out of doors. No fresh air at all. It can't be good for him. Does John play squash?
[EVELYN. No.
DIANA. Oh.
EVELYN. He doesn't play anything.]
Oh, well. He probably doesn't need it. Exercise. Some men don't. My father never took a stroke of exercise. Till he died. He seemed fit enough. He managed to do what he wanted to do. Mind you, he never did very much. He just used to sit and shout at we girls. Most of the time. He got calmer though when he got older. After my mother left him.

(*Looking into the pram.*) Did you knit that little jacket for him?

[EVELYN. No.]

Pretty. (*Pause.*) No, there are times when I think that's the principal trouble between Paul and me. I mean, I know now I'm running myself down but Paul basically, he's got much more go – well, I mean let's face it, he's much cleverer than me. Let's face it. Basically. I mean, I was the bright one in our family but I can't keep up with Paul sometimes. When he has one of his moods, I think to myself, now if I was really clever, I could probably talk him round or something but I mean the thing is, really and truly, and I know I'm running myself down when I say this, I don't think I'm really enough for him. He needs me, I can tell that; he doesn't say as much but I know he does. It's just, as I say, I don't think I'm really enough for him. (*She reflects.*) But he couldn't do without me. Make no mistake about that. He's got this amazing energy. I don't know where he finds it. He goes to bed long after me, he's up at dawn, working down here – then off he goes all day . . . I need my eight hours, it's no good. What I'm saying is really, I wouldn't blame him. Not altogether. If he did. With someone else. You know, another woman. I wouldn't blame him, I wouldn't blame her. Not as long as I was told. Providing I know, that I'm told – all right. Providing I feel able to say to people – 'Yes, I am well aware that my husband is having an affair with such and such or whoever . . . it's quite all right. I know all about it. We're both grown-up people, we know what we're doing, he knows I know, she knows I know. So mind your own business.' I'd feel all right about it. But I will not stand deception. I'm simply asking that I be told. Either by him or if not by her. Not necessarily now but sometime. You see. (*A pause.* EVELYN *is expressionless.*). I know he is, you see. He's not very clever and he's a very bad liar like most men. If he takes the trouble, like last Saturday, to tell me he's just going down the road to the football match, he might at least

2

choose a day when they're playing at home. (*She lifts the tablecloth and inspects the sandwiches.*) I hope I've made enough tomato. No, I must be told. Otherwise it makes my life impossible. I can't talk to anybody without them . . . I expect them, both of them, at least to have some feeling for me. (*She blows her nose.*) Well. (*The doorbell rings.*) Excuse me . . .

COMMENTARY: *Absent Friends*, like so many of Ayckbourn's best early plays, is a comedy of modern manners. Behind the surface humour is a shrewd analysis of suburban mores, disillusion and despair. Ayckbourn is skilled at creating situations and characters that have both comic and sad elements which reveal the pain of everyday life and blighted relationships. The put-upon women in Ayckbourn's plays are presented with understanding and compassion. In *Absent Friends* the issues of death and deceit are given a laughable gloss. This is a darkly hilarious play.

Diana launches into her monologue with the 'expressionless' Evelyn as her audience. This is a one-way conversation. Diana is a compulsive talker. She volleys a torrent of words against an unyielding wall of silence. Notice how she keeps trying to redefine what she says, peppering her speech with phrases like 'I mean' and 'What I'm saying is really'. It also becomes an exorcism for her: a way to expel the demon fears and anxieties about her own inadequacy and her husband's infidelity. Like so many of Ayckbourn's heroines she has a palpable fear of sickness and death, divorce and adultery. Her frame of reference seems entirely culled from the pages of women's magazines. To the outside world she wants to maintain the illusion of a happy marriage; keeping up appearances is vital for her even if her marriage is in reality a sad sham. Diana's neurotic insecurity and constant self-deprecation hints at the breakdown she will experience later in the play. She suspects Paul's adultery and fears losing him. Ayckbourn portrays Paul as a vain, egoistic and selfish man, but in Diana's eyes he has all the qualities of a suburban hero. When Diana opens the play with this speech it is not clear whether she knows for certain that it is Evelyn who is having the affair with Paul. You might want to consider how knowledge, suspicion or ignorance of this crucial fact might affect your delivery of the speech. Is Diana just talking randomly to anyone within earshot or directing her words specifically at Evelyn with a menacing intent? There is a significant age difference between the two women: Evelyn is younger, trendier, heavily made-up and expressionless. Diana, who changes expressions and tone throughout the speech, might be measuring herself against this sphinx-like rival. Despite all the sadness revealed in the speech, the actor should follow Diana's example and keep up a resolutely chatty and cheerful exterior.

After the Fall

(1964) Arthur Miller

Act 1. A bare stage.

Holga (30s) is a German archaeologist. She is a calm and independent woman. But the past haunts her. Here she reminisces about the war.

HOLGA. It was the middle of the war. I had just come out of a class and there were leaflets on the sidewalk. A photograph of a concentration camp. And emaciated people. It was dropped there by British Intelligence; one tended to believe the British. I had no idea. Truly. Any more, perhaps, than Americans know how a Negro lives. I was seventeen; I lived in my studies; I planned how to cut my hair differently. It is much more complicated than it seems later. There were many officers in my family. It was our country. It isn't easy to turn against your country; not in a war. There are always reasons – do Americans turn against America because of Hiroshima? No, there are reasons always. (*Pause.*) And I took the leaflet to my godfather – he was still commanding our Intelligence. And I asked if it were true. 'Of course,' he said, 'why does it excite you?' And I said, 'You are a swine. You are all swine.' I threw my briefcase at him. And he opened it and put some papers in and asked me to deliver it to a certain address. And I became a courier for the officers who were planning to assassinate Hitler. . . . They were all hanged.
[QUENTIN. Why not you?
HOLGA. They didn't betray me.
QUENTIN. Then why do you say good faith is never sure?]
(*After a pause.*) It was my country . . . longer perhaps than it

5

should have been. But I didn't know. And now I don't know how I could not have known. I can't imagine not knowing, now.

COMMENTARY: Miller's *After the Fall* is a play about how guilt preys heavily on innocent minds. Within the framework of the play the Second World War represents a fall from grace. Anyone touched by those times, whether in Germany or elsewhere, has been compromised. So it is with Holga who reveals how she first became aware of evil as a young student in Nazi Germany.

Holga's speech discloses the clear memory of a moral and political turning point in her life. A chance encounter with a leaflet outside a school yard sets off the chain of related incidents that grow into a plot, in which she is involved, to assassinate Adolf Hitler. Although Holga does not describe the photograph of the concentration camp her reaction to it justifies everything that follows. Try to imagine or find the kind of image that would have this impact. Notice how calmly Holga relates her transition from innocent ignorance to knowledge, from passive indifference to active involvement. Although the speech seems very neutral and matter-of-fact, it is also an admission of collective guilt and a confession. Holga speaks slowly and simply. Her command of English is precise and functional. She has a rational, scientific mind (she is an archaeologist) so she speaks clearly. The actor must find a way to convey her quiet passion and strong compassion. She concludes her speech on a note of uncertainty. Despite all that she has experienced she realizes there can be no moral victories.

Antigone
(1944) Jean Anouilh

Scene 1. Set without historical or geographical connotations. Vaguely Greek but more modern.

Antigone (20) is the daughter of the late King Oedipus and lives with her older sister, Ismene, in the house of their uncle, King Creon. She is engaged to Haemon, Creon's son. Her two brothers Eteocles and Polynices kill one another in a duel, each trying to gain control of Thebes. Creon orders that Eteocles is to be buried with full honours and declares Polynices a rebel, forbidding his burial. Antigone, believing it is her duty to honour Polynices, buries him herself with all the appropriate rituals but she is caught by Creon's guards. In this scene Creon offers to murder the guards and suppress all news of her crime if she agrees both to maintain silence about it and obey him. She responds to his offer with this speech, revealing her uncompromising integrity.

ANTIGONE (*softly*). And what will my happiness be like? What kind of a happy woman will Antigone grow into? What base things will she have to do, day after day, in order to snatch her own little scrap of happiness? Tell me – who will she have to lie to? Smile at? Sell herself to? Who will she have to avert her eyes from, and leave to die?
[CREON. That's enough. You're crazy.]
I won't be quiet! I want to know what I have to do to be happy! Now, right away, because now is when I have to choose. You say life's so wonderful. I want to know what I have to do to live.
[CREON. Do you love Haemon?]
I love a Haemon who's tough and young . . . A Haemon who's demanding and loyal, like me. But if that life of yours, that happiness of yours, are going to pass over him and erode

7

him – if he's not going to turn pale any more when I turn pale
– if he won't think I must be dead if I'm five minutes late – if
he doesn't feel alone in the world and hate me if I laugh and
he doesn't know why – if he's going to become just a
conventional spouse and learn to say yes like the rest – then
no, I don't love Haemon any more!

[CREON. That'll do. You don't know what you're saying.]
I know what I'm saying, all right! It's just that you don't
understand. I'm speaking to you from too far away now –
from a country you can't enter any more, with your
wrinkles, your wisdom and your belly. (*Laughs.*) I suddenly
see you as you were when you were fifteen! Helpless, but
thinking you're important. All life has added are those
furrows in your face, that fat around your waist!

[CREON (*shaking her*). Will you shut up!]
Why do you want to shut me up? Because you know I'm
right? Don't you think I can see it in your eyes? You know
I'm right, but you'll never admit it because you're trying to
defend that happiness of yours – like a dog crouching over a
bone.

[CREON. Your happiness as well as mine, you fool!]
You disgust me, all of you, you and your happiness! And
your life, that has to be loved at any price. You're like dogs
fawning on everyone they come across. With just a little
hope left every day – if you don't expect too much. But I
want everything, now! And to the full! Or else I decline the
offer, lock, stock and barrel! I want to be sure of having
everything, now, this very day, and it has to be as wonderful
as it was when I was little. Otherwise I prefer to die.

Translation by Barbara Bray

COMMENTARY: Anouilh's modern version of *Antigone* was a
conscious attempt to cloak in myth the dilemma facing the French
people during the World War II occupation by the Nazis. By

camouflaging his ideas behind a well-known classical tale, the dramatist was able to explore freely the moral ambiguity posed by collaboration with the enemy. In this play Antigone prefers to die rather than compromise her integrity in a morally corrupt world. Today the play is frequently revived. The conflict and debate between Antigone and Creon have lost none of their impact or relevance. As with all Anouilh's plays it provides actors with well-crafted roles and eminently speakable dialogue that forces the audience to listen.

Antigone is a modern young woman. She is angry and challenging not only towards her uncle – a father surrogate – but towards all notions of authority that block free will and happiness. The emotionally charged knowledge that both her brothers are dead and that her own life is in the balance must influence each of her words. Her entire speech is about individual liberation and living without imposed limitations. Unlike her precursor in classical Greek tragedy, who was driven by religious principle and a sense of justice, this Antigone is a selfish, wilful and stubborn individualist. Her goal is her own happiness. Antigone hammers away at Creon and even takes some glee in the fact that she can arouse his anger. You might notice how she preys on Creon's age and paunch. Even though a dictator, Creon sounds perfectly reasonable. He is not a butcher, never speaks of concentration camps or cruelty. He wants an orderly state of affairs. Antigone can see his blind spots. She uses her mocking, sarcastic speeches to castigate and cross-examine Creon, and provoke his anger. Notice how she hurls his own words and phrases back in his face. As she finally says she would 'prefer to die' and just say 'no' than be denied happiness by living according to Creon's dictates.

The Balcony
(1956) Jean Genet

Scene 5. Irma's room, an elegant boudoir with lace hangings, dressing table and gilded mirror.

Irma 'is about forty, dark, severe-looking, and is wearing a black tailored suit'. She is the Madame of a brothel and has been going over her accounts. She is talking to one of her girls, Carmen, explaining how she realizes her clients' fantasies.

IRMA. They all want everything to be as real as possible. . . . Minus something indefinable, so that it won't be real. (*Changing her tone.*) Carmen, it was I who decided to call my establishment a house of illusions, but I'm only the manager. Each individual, when he rings the bell and enters, brings his own scenario, perfectly thought out. My job is merely to rent the hall and furnish the props, actors and actresses. My dear, I've succeeded in lifting it from the ground – do you see what I mean? I unloosed it long ago and it's flying. I cut the moorings. It's flying. Or, if you like, it's sailing in the sky, and I with it. Well, my darling . . . may I say something tender – every madame always, traditionally, has a slight partiality for one of her young ladies. . . .
[CARMEN. I had noticed it, Madame, and I too, at times. . . . (*She looks at* IRMA *languidly.*)]
(*Stands up and looks at her.*) I have a strange feeling, Carmen. (*A long pause.*) But let's continue. Darling, the house really does take off, leaves the earth, sails in the sky when, in the secrecy of my heart, I call myself, but with great precision, a keeper of a bawdy-house. Darling, when secretly, in silence, I repeat to myself silently, 'You're a bawd, boss of a
10

whorehouse,' darling everything (*Suddenly lyrical.*) flies off – chandeliers, mirrors, carpets, pianos, caryatids and my studios, my famous studios: the Hay Studio, hung with rustic scenes, the Studio of the Hangings, spattered with blood and tears, the Throne-room Studio, draped in velvet with a *fleur-de-lis* pattern, the Studio of Mirrors, the Studio of State, the Studio of the Scented Fountains, the Urinal Studio, the Amphitrite Studio, the Funeral Studio, adorned with marble urns, the Moonlight Studio, everything flies off: studios – Oh! I was forgetting the studio of the beggars, of the tramps, where filth and poverty are magnified. To continue: studios, girls, crystals, laces, balconies, everything skedaddles, rises up and carries me away!

Translation by Bernard Frechtman

COMMENTARY: Genet's *The Balcony* continues to be a lurid and fascinating exercise in the powers of role playing and self-delusion. In the world of the play illusion has far more power than reality. It is set in a brothel where a group of whores and their clients play out profane fantasies of mock nobility. Good and evil are twinned throughout the play. Both sides are on display simultaneously. Each character is stretched between these two moral poles as though pinioned on a torture rack.

Irma is an intriguing combination of vamp and hard-nosed businesswoman. She is both a sexual creature and a practical stage manageress. She knows how to create and decorate every man's (and woman's) fantasy. Unless the actor is willing to give full flight to Irma's illusions this speech simply will not work. Notice that Irma literally lets her imagination take flight. Irma seduces her victims by transporting them to a different realm; as she says at the top of her speech: 'you want everything to be as real as possible'. The sheer theatricality of the monologue, however, should always hint that nothing Irma says is real at all. Genet's infinite juxtaposition of illusion and reality must be playfully apparent to the audience. Irma must seem like some sort of camp interior decorator with that certain touch for satisfying her clients' every wish. The actor must decide how to interpret Irma's overtly flirtatious attitude towards 'darling' Carmen in the middle of the speech. She describes everything with great pride with an eye to impressing Carmen. The speech is highly sensual and full of tactile touches. As Irma's enthusiasm builds her words reach a crescendo of theatrical delight.

The Bald Prima Donna
(1950) Eugène Ionesco

One act. A typical middle-class English interior.

Mrs Smith (middle-aged) is married to Mr Smith. As the play opens they are enjoying a 'typical English evening at home'. 'Typical English' Mr Smith is sitting in his favourite armchair. 'Next to him, in her favourite armchair, typically English Mrs Smith is darning English socks. A long English silence. An English clock chimes three English chimes.'

MRS SMITH. Goodness! Nine o'clock! This evening for supper we had soup, fish, cold ham and mashed potatoes and a good English salad, and we had English beer to drink. The children drank English water. We had a very good meal this evening. And that's because we are English, because we live in a suburb of London and because our name is Smith. (MR SMITH *goes on reading his newspaper and clicks his tongue.*) Mashed potatoes are very nice with cold ham. The mayonnaise was quite fresh. The mayonnaise from the grocer round the corner is much better quality than the mayonnaise from the grocer opposite, it's even better than the mayonnaise from the grocer at the bottom of the hill. Of course I don't mean to say that his mayonnaise is bad . . . (MR SMITH, *still reading, clicks his tongue.*) Yet the fact remains that the mayonnaise from the grocer round the corner is best . . . (MR SMITH, *still reading, clicks his tongue.*) Mary did the potatoes very well for once. Last time she didn't do them at all well. I only like them when they're done nicely. (MR SMITH, *still reading, clicks his tongue.*) The fish was nice and fresh. It makes my mouth water to think of it. I took two

13

helpings. No, three! And it always gives me the colly-wobbles. *You* took three helpings, too. But the third time you took less than the first two times, and *I* took a lot more. I had more to eat than you did this evening. How did that come about? You don't usually suffer from lack of appetite. (MR SMITH, *still reading, clicks his tongue.*) Our little boy did so want to drink some beer tonight; he'll be fond of a glass or two, when he's older; he takes after you, dear. Did you see him at table, how he couldn't take his eyes off the bottle? But I picked up the jug and poured out a glass of water. He drank it because he was thirsty. Helen takes after me: she's a good little housewife, very economical and she plays the piano. She never asks to be allowed to drink English beer. Neither does our youngest little girl, who lives on bread and milk. Anyone can tell she's only two years old. Her name is Peggy. The elderberry tart was excellent. Perhaps with the dessert we should have had a little glass of Australian Burgundy, but I didn't put the wine on the table, so as not to set the children a bad example. We must bring them up not to be wild and extravagant. (MR SMITH, *still reading, clicks his tongue.*) Mrs Parker goes to a Rumanian grocer called Popesco-Rosenfeld, who's just arrived from Constantinople. He's a specialist in yoghurt. He holds a diploma from a school for yoghurticians in Andrinopolis. I think I'll pay him a visit tomorrow and buy a great big pot of real home-made Rumanian yoghurt. It's not often one gets the chance of finding such things here in the suburbs of London. (MR SMITH, *still reading, clicks his tongue.*) Yoghurt is very good for the stomach, the lumbar regions, appendicitis and apotheosis. At least, that's what Dr Mack-enzie-King told me, you know, the one who looks after the Johns' children, the people next door. He's a fine doctor. One can always have faith in what he tells you. He never prescribes anything he hasn't first tried out on himself. Before he made Parker go through that operation last year, he had himself operated on, for liver, you know, although there was nothing wrong with him at the time.

Translation by Donald Watson

COMMENTARY: Ionesco's *The Bald Prima Donna* is a benchmark in the development of modern drama. It presents a savage parody of English suburbia with puppet-like characters parroting simplistic cliches, banal opinions and non-sequiturs. Ionesco's fractured absurdity, which seemed so radical and innovative in 1950, strikes us today as something straight out of a Monty Python routine.

Mrs Smith is not a real character but a caricature, a living stereotype. How to act a stereotype is part of the challenge here. Her speech is about mundanity turned inside out until it transforms itself into a kind of madness. The humour in this piece cannot be forced. It comes of its own accord as Mrs Smith's litany of commonplace observations, which ought to read like a shopping list, accumulate into a heaping mound of treacly triteness. The speech is about feeding. Mrs Smith spoon-feeds Mr Smith (and the audience) a rich diet of inane chatter. Yet midway through the monologue something bizarre happens. The mundane transmutes into something exotic with the appearance of Popesco-Rosenfeld, the Rumanian grocer and yoghurtician. We have radically shifted from a typical suburban 'English' setting to an East European realm where there are 'schools of yoghurticians'! The actor delivering this speech has got to be sly with the humour. Mrs Smith is deadpan but also alive to the jokiness of a doctor who will operate on himself just to see what it feels like. With this speech you are inventing for the audience odd, surreal images that have been released from their normal moorings.

Blithe Spirit
(1941) Noël Coward

Act 2, scene 2. The living-room of the Condomines' house in Kent. Late afternoon.

Ruth Condomine 'is a smart-looking woman in the middle thirties'. She and her husband, Charles, have both been previously married. At a seance led by Madame Arcati, an eccentric psychic, the spirit of Charles' first wife Elvira appears, but only Charles can see or hear her. Elvira refuses to return to the spirit world without Charles. Ruth although initially sceptical of Elvira's presence grudgingly and jealously acknowledges her. Here she confronts Charles and, indirectly, Elvira. (Following this is a speech by Elvira herself.)

RUTH (*furiously*). I've been doing my level best to control myself ever since yesterday morning and I'm damned if I'm going to try any more, the strain is too much. She has the advantage of being able to say whatever she pleases without me being able to hear her, but she can hear me all right, can't she, without any modified interpreting? . . . You haven't told me what she really said – you wouldn't dare. Judging from her photograph she's the type who would use most unpleasant language . . . I've been making polite conversation all through dinner last night and breakfast and lunch today – and it's been a nightmare – and I am not going to do it any more. I don't like Elvira any more than she likes me and what's more I'm certain that I never could have, dead or alive. If, since her untimely arrival here the other evening, she had shown the slightest sign of good manners, the slightest sign of breeding, I might have felt differently towards her, but all she has done is try to make mischief between us and have private jokes with you against me. I am

16

now going up to my room and I shall have my dinner on a tray. You and she can have the house to yourselves and joke and gossip with each other to your heart's content. The first thing in the morning I am going up to London to interview the Psychical Research Society and if they fail me I shall go straight to the Archbishop of Canterbury.

COMMENTARY: Noël Coward's best plays are drawing-room comedies where triangular relationships – modern love affairs – ultimately break down due to jealousies. His characters try desperately hard to present a mask of urbane accommodation. When they reach the breaking point then their hearts overrule their heads. In *Blithe Spirit* the world beyond collides with the here and now resulting in hilarious consequences.

Ruth's speech shatters her elegant façade of dignity. She has, as she says, finally reached the breaking point and this is her ultimatum to Charles. Her voice betrays the strain of resentment, jealousy and humiliation. Elvira is her rival in every way, aided by the fact that she is invisible and able to wreak havoc. There is a description of Elvira in the Commentary for the following speech, which should help you understand Ruth's attitude to her. Notice that all her statements are well-crafted declarative sentences. Ruth witheringly refers to Elvira as 'she,' only using her name once. The actor might consider letting her anger build and finally releasing it on the high Anglican tones of 'Archbishop of Canterbury'. The danger here is letting your anger peak too soon. Fight to keep under control. Ruth is a civilised creature who, unexpectedly, loses her normal coolness and civility out of jealousy.

Act 3, scene 1. A few days later. After dinner.

Elvira (20s) 'is charmingly dressed in a sort of negligée. Everything about her is grey; hair, skin, dress, hands, so we must accept the fact that she is not quite of this world'. She died seven years ago in a boating accident. Before her death Elvira had been married to the novelist Charles Condomine. Elvira's plan, to murder Charles so that he will return with her to the spirit world, backfires and Ruth, rather than Charles, is killed in the car accident Elvira engineers. Realizing she has failed, Elvira wants to return to the spirit world. When Charles pours scorn on her plans, calling her 'unscrupulous,' she bursts into 'ghost tears' as she starts this speech.

ELVIRA. That's right – rub it in. Anyhow it was only because I love you – the silliest thing I ever did in my whole life was to love you – you were always unworthy of me.
[CHARLES. That remark comes perilously near impertinence, Elvira.]
I sat there, on the other side, just longing for you day after day. I did really – all through your affair with that brassy-looking woman in the South of France I went on loving you and thinking truly of you – then you married Ruth and even then I forgave you and tried to understand because all the time I believed deep inside that you really loved me best . . . that's why I put myself down for a return visit and had to fill in all those forms and wait about in draughty passages for hours – if only you'd died before you met Ruth everything might have been all right – she's absolutely ruined you – I hadn't been in the house a day before I realized that. Your books aren't a quarter as good as they used to be either.

COMMENTARY: Elvira is the opposite of Ruth (*see above*). She is winsome, childlike and capricious. Everything about her suggests she is ornamental. Charles says of Elvira: 'I remember her very distinctly indeed – I remember how fascinating she was, and how maddening – I remember how badly she played all games and how cross she got when she didn't win – I remember her gay charm when she had achieved her own way over something and her extreme acidity when she didn't – I remember her physical attractiveness, which was tremendous, and her spiritual integrity which was nil.' Something about Elvira seems to have changed as a result of her time in the spirit world. A harder, more resentful woman is the one the audience hears now. She tries to make Charles feel guilty as she artfully details her selfless devotion to him. While still alive Elvira was 'wickedly unfaithful' so you must decide how honest she is at this point. The actor might want to notice how Elvira uses 'I' and 'you' with great manipulative effect. She portrays herself as the wronged heroine, willing to turn a blind eye to all Charles' peccadilloes. In true Elvira fashion it is all a bit over the top, and she ends the speech in a typically petulant mood.

Blues for Mister Charlie

(1964) James Baldwin

Act 3. Juanita's bedroom. An unnamed town in the deep South. Early Sunday morning.

Juanita (20s) is an independent black activist student who plans to go up north to law school. Her former boyfriend, Richard Henry, returns to town after eight years in New York where he was working as a singer. They start seeing one another again and even plan to marry. However, Richard is murdered by a white shopkeeper who is then brought to trial. In this monologue Juanita describes her love affair with Richard.

JUANITA (*rises from bed*). He lay beside me on that bed like a rock. As heavy as a rock – like he'd fallen – fallen from a high place – fallen so far and landed so heavy, he seemed almost to be sinking out of sight – with one knee pointing to heaven. My God. He covered me like that. He wasn't at all like I thought he was. He fell on – fell on me – like life and death. My God. His chest, his belly, the rising and the falling, the moans. How he clung, how he struggled – life and death! Life and death! Why did it all seem to me like tears? That he came to me, clung to me, plunged into me, sobbing, howling, bleeding, somewhere inside his chest, his belly, and it all came out, came pouring out, like tears! My God, the smell, the touch, the taste, the sound of anguish! Richard! Why couldn't I have held you closer? Held you, held you, borne you, given you life again! Oh, Richard. The teeth that gleamed, oh! when you smiled, the spit flying when you cursed, the teeth stinging when you bit – your breath, your hands, your weight, my God, when you moved in me! Where shall I go now, what shall I do? Oh. Oh. Oh.

20

Mama was frightened. Frightened because little Juanita brought her first real lover to this house. I suppose God does for Mama what Richard did for me. Juanita! I don't care! I don't care! Yes, I want a lover made of flesh and blood, of flesh and blood, like me, I don't want to be God's mother! He can *have* His icy, snow-white heaven! If He is somewhere around this fearful planet, if I ever see Him, I will spit in His face! In God's face! How *dare* He presume to judge a living soul! A living soul. Mama is afraid I'm pregnant. Mama is afraid of so much. I'm not afraid. I hope I'm pregnant. I *hope* I am! One more illegitimate black baby – that's right, you jive mothers! And I am going to raise my baby to be a man. A *man*, you dig? Oh, let me be pregnant, let me be pregnant, don't let it all be gone! A man. Juanita. A man. Oh, my God, there are no more. For me. Did this happen to Mama sometime? Did she have a man sometime who vanished like smoke? And left her to get through this world as best she could? Is that why she married my father? Did this happen to Mother Henry? Is this how we all get to be mothers – so soon? of helpless men – because all the other men perish? No. No. No. No. What is this world like? I will end up taking care of some man, some day. Help me do it with love. Pete. Meridian. Parnell. We have been the mothers for them all. It must be dreadful to be Parnell. There is no flesh he can touch. All of it is bloody. Incest everywhere. Ha-ha! You're going crazy, Juanita. Oh, Lord, don't let me go mad. Let me be pregnant! Let me be pregnant!

COMMENTARY: James Baldwin's *Blues for Mister Charlie* revolves around a racial murder. It evokes a time and place in America when the tension between whites and blacks was at its fiercest. During the 1960s Baldwin's writing became synonymous with the struggle for black rights and the declaration of a black voice in drama. Like so many modern American plays it is about a journey and about outsiders. *Blues for Mister Charlie* is one of Baldwin's most lyrical creations, revealing a great humanity and an uncompromising honesty. If you compare his writing with that of, say, Athol Fugard (*see page 53*) you'll notice a close kinship. Their characters are representative of an underclass; individuals caught in the crossfire of hatred and racial resentment.

Juanita is a character who finds herself suddenly at the very centre of a struggle, with both a public and private resonance. Through her relationship with Richard and the love shown to her by Parnell, a white man, she becomes embroiled in both a sexual and racial conflict. Her monologue describes her last moments of intimacy and lovemaking with Richard. She describes his heavy, solid body as if it were a corpse. It prefigures Richard's mortal wounding both figuratively and literally. This is not a romantic tryst she is recounting but a life and death struggle. The word 'struggle' is key to this monologue. It underscores the tension and fear Juanita is feeling. Notice the evocative words and images she uses as she lyrically and boldly narrates their lovemaking. The actor can let the rhythm of her language, the 'rising' and 'falling', propel her through this demanding speech. It is full of physical writhings. She is remembering a specific moment, trying to convey its sensual and emotional impact. For Juanita this is a complex memory laced with guilt, love, anger and regret. The hope that she is pregnant and filled with a new life elates her. She ends the speech on a crest of transporting fervour and passion. The monologue has the rhythmic pulsing quality of a blues serenade.

Cat on a Hot Tin Roof

(1955) Tennessee Williams

Act 1. The bed-sitting room of a plantation home in the Mississippi Delta.

Margaret ('Maggie') is a 'pretty young woman, with anxious lines in her face . . . [her] voice is both rapid and drawling. In her long speeches she has the vocal tricks of a priest delivering a liturgical chant, the lines are almost sung, always continuing a little beyond her breath so she has to gasp for another. Sometimes she intersperses the lines with a little wordless singing, such as "Da-da-daa!"' She is wearing 'a slip of ivory satin and lace . . . Her voice has range, and music sometimes it drops low as a boy's and you have a sudden image of her playing boys' games as a child'. She lives with her husband Brick, in the house of his father, Big Daddy. Maggie delights in sensuality, but her marriage to Brick (who only later confesses to his homosexuality) has been sexless, passionless and childless. In this scene Maggie is talking to Brick, who is lying on their bed with a broken leg, about his family and their rivalry with Gooper (Brother Man) and his threatening brood.

MARGARET. Big Daddy dotes on you, honey. And he can't stand Brother Man and Brother Man's wife, that monster of fertility, Mae. Know how I know? By little expressions that flicker over his face when that woman is holding fo'th on one of her choice topics such as – how she refused twilight sleep – when the twins were delivered! Because she feels motherhood's an experience that a woman ought to experience fully! – in order to fully appreciate the wonder and beauty of it! HAH! – and how she made Brother Man come in an' stand beside her in the delivery room so he would not miss out on the 'wonder and beauty' of it either! – producin' those no-neck monsters. . . . (*A speech of this kind*

23

would be antipathetic from almost anybody but MARGARET; *she makes it oddly funny, because her eyes constantly twinkle and her voice shakes with laughter which is basically indulgent.*) – Big Daddy shares my attitude toward those two! As for me, well – I give him a laugh now and then and he tolerates me. In fact! – I sometimes suspect that Big Daddy harbours a little unconscious 'lech' fo' me. . . .

[BRICK. What makes you think that Big Daddy has a lech for you, Maggie?]

Way he always drops his eyes down my body when I'm talkin' to him, drops his eyes to my boobs an' licks his old chops! Ha ha!

[BRICK. That kind of talk is disgusting.]

Did anyone ever tell you that you're an ass-aching Puritan, Brick? I think it's mighty fine that the ole fellow, on the doorstep of death, still takes in my shape with what I think is deserved appreciation! And you wanta know something else? Big Daddy didn't know how many little Maes and Goopers had been produced! 'How many kids have you got?' he asked at the table, just like Brother Man and his wife were new acquaintances to him! Big Mama said he was jokin', but that ole boy wasn't jokin', Lord, no! And when they infawmed him that they had five already and were turning out number six! – the news seemed to come as a sort of unpleasant surprise . . . (*Children yell below.*) *Scream, monsters!* (*Turns to* BRICK *with a sudden, gay, charming smile which fades as she notices that he is not looking at her but into fading gold space with a troubled expression. It is constant rejection that makes her humour 'bitchy'.*) Yes, you should of been at that supper-table, Baby. (*Whenever she calls him 'baby' the word is a soft caress.*) Y'know, Big Daddy, bless his ole sweet soul, he's the dearest ole thing in the whole world, but he does hunch over his food as if he preferred not to notice anything else. Well, Mae an' Gooper were side by side at the table, direckly across from Big Daddy, watchin' his face like hawks while they jawed an' jabbered about the

24

cuteness an' brilliance of th' no-neck monsters! (*She giggles with a hand fluttering at her throat and her breast and her long throat arched. She comes downstage and recreates the scene with voice and gesture.*) And the no-neck monsters were ranged around the table, some in high chairs and on th' *Books of Knowledge*, all in fancy little paper caps in honour of Big Daddy's birthday, and all through dinner, well, I want you to know that Brother man an' his partner never once, for one moment, stopped exchanging pokes an' pinches an' kicks an' signs an' signals! – Why, they were like a couple of cardsharps fleecing a sucker. – Even Big Mama, bless her ole sweet soul, she isn't th' quickest an' brightest thing in the world, she finally noticed, at last, an' said to Gooper, 'Gooper, what are you an' Mae makin' all these signs at each other about?' – I swear t' goodness, I nearly choked on my chicken!

COMMENTARY: After four decades Williams' *Cat on a Hot Tin Roof* still manages to seethe with life. 'Maggie the Cat' is a character who has attracted actresses as various as Elizabeth Taylor, Natalie Wood, Lindsay Duncan and Kathleen Turner. The playwright's own vivid description of her (included in the introduction and stage directions above) hint at a feminine, feline presence who is as provoking as she is provocative. This is a potently physical speech.

Margaret is, by turns, taunting, soothing, 'bitchy', seductive, destructive, purring, humorous and caustic. Like a skittery alley cat she scents and shifts at the slightest mood change. She is uneasy in her own skin and literally prowls around the room, taking the measure of her indifferent mate. She is also hot and clammy. Right from the very first line ('Big Daddy dotes on you, honey.') Margaret fills every nook and cranny of the stage with her rich, colloquial speech and her laugh. Notice, also, how the playwright has made his character a creature of slang. She is not afraid to be vulgar but relishes the opportunity to show her rural Southern spirit. Her speech is sung like an aria. Like so many of

Tennessee Williams' heroines, Maggie is an irrepressible life force. The dramatist gives her loaded words to work with; many of them, like 'lech,' are sexual double entendres and practically every word she speaks can be bent in this direction. Her effort throughout the speech is to draw a reaction from the silent Brick, who only interrupts her twice. Pushing and pulling is what Maggie does through words. Look carefully at the speech and you'll discover its themes: fertility and children. Maggie and Brick have none; the hateful Mae and Gooper have five already, with a sixth on the way. An heir has to be produced. So Maggie's cattiness has a genuine source. The description of Mae and Gooper's children as 'no-neck monsters' shifts the speech into the realm of the comic grotesque. The parents themselves are described as birds of prey, waiting to pounce on the family fortune. Maggie and Brick are in the privacy of their own bedroom, and practically naked. So what she says cuts very close to the bone. Nothing Maggie says or does is restrained. Throughout the speech she displays herself from every angle; not only to Brick but to the audience. She goes after her husband tooth and claw looking for tender bits of flesh that will show her scratches.

Cloud Nine
(1979) Caryl Churchill

Act 2, scene 4. A London park on a late summer afternoon.

Betty (40–50) has two grown-up children and works as a receptionist in a doctor's surgery. She lives alone having recently separated from her husband, Clive.

BETTY. I used to think Clive was the one who liked sex. But then I found I missed it. I used to touch myself when I was very little, I thought I'd invented something wonderful. I used to do it to go to sleep with or to cheer myself up, and one day it was raining and I was under the kitchen table, and my mother saw me with my hand under my dress rubbing away, and she dragged me out so quickly I hit my head and it bled and I was sick, and nothing was said, and I never did it again till this year. I thought if Clive wasn't looking at me there wasn't a person there. And one night in bed in my flat I was so frightened I started touching myself. I thought my hand might go through space. I touched my face, it was there, my arm, my breast, and my hand went down where I thought it shouldn't, and I thought well there is somebody there. It felt very sweet, it was a feeling from very long ago, it was very soft, just barely touching, and I felt myself gathering more and more and I felt angry with Clive and angry with my mother and I went on defying them, and there was this vast feeling growing in me and all round me and they couldn't stop me and no one could stop me and I was there and coming and coming. Afterwards I thought I'd betrayed Clive. My mother would kill me. But I felt triumphant because I was a separate person from them. And

27

I cried because I didn't want to be. But I don't cry about it any more. Sometimes I do it three times in one night and it really is great fun.

COMMENTARY: When it first appeared in London and New York, Caryl Churchill's *Cloud Nine* made an instant impact. It is a play about sexual fantasies fulfilled and unfulfilled; the reversals of history and genders. The lines of conflict are clearly drawn between the anxiety of staying within a defined social role and the liberation experienced when stereotypical guises are suddenly dropped.

This is a very candid speech that should catch the listener unawares and make him or her shift their perspective. Betty takes the audience into her confidence with this revelation. There is nothing overtly political or declamatory about Betty. The speech works best when her disclosures sound almost matter of fact. What she says, after all, is quite natural. She is never graphic in her descriptions; she is not trying to shock. From all appearances she is a suburban wife and mother. Betty's single act of liberation, through masturbation, is both a purgative and cure for a restless soul. She literally discovers herself and her personal sexual history in this speech. She realizes that she's separate from everyone else and can gratify herself whenever she pleases. This is an intimate confession of sensual and personal freedom.

The Cocktail Party
(1950) T. S. Eliot

Act 1, scene 2. The drawing-room of the Chamberlaynes' London flat. Evening.

Celia Coplestone (20s) is having an affair with the married and middle-aged Edward Chamberlayne. At a cocktail party which he is hosting, Edward tells Celia that he wants to end their affair. He tries to explain his reasons, claiming that although he loves her he feels he is too old to continue the relationship. He also admits that he cannot really explain his motives. Celia, realizing that she no longer feels the same way about Edward, gives her reaction in this speech.

CELIA. I am not sure, Edward, that I understand you;
And yet I understand as I never did before.
I think – I believe – you are being yourself
As you never were before, with me.
Twice you have changed since I have been looking at you.
I looked at your face: and I thought that I knew
And loved every contour; and as I looked
It withered, as if I had unwrapped a mummy.
I listened to your voice, that had always thrilled me,
And it became another voice – no, not a voice;
What I heard was only the noise of an insect,
Dry, endless, meaningless, inhuman –
You might have made it by scraping your legs together –
Or however grasshoppers do it. I looked,
And listened for your heart, your blood;
And saw only a beetle the size of a man
With nothing more inside it than what comes out
When you tread on a beetle.
[EDWARD.   Perhaps that is what I am.

Tread on me, if you like.]
                              No, I won't tread on you.
That is not what you are. It is only what was left
Of what I had thought you were. I see another person,
I see you as a person whom I never saw before.
The man I saw before, he was only a projection –
I see that now – of something that I wanted –
No, not *wanted* – something I aspired to –
Something that I desperately wanted to exist.
It must happen somewhere – but what, and where is it?
Edward, I see that I was simply making use of you.
And I ask you to forgive me.

COMMENTARY: Eliot's *The Cocktail Party*, you'll instantly notice, is a modern drawing-room play written entirely in blank verse. On the surface it is a sophisticated comedy about romance and infidelity, while underneath it is full of religious symbols and psychological torment that transform it into a modern humanistic morality play.

The actor must simply forget that the speech is written in verse. Treat it entirely as natural, conversational speech and it will work very easily when spoken aloud. That is what the playwright intended. All the sounds and rhythms of modern speech are present in the lines. Phrases, you'll see, have already been broken down into speakable units. The very specific length of each line means that you can aim the words more accurately at the audience. The speech contains a detailed observation and analysis of Edward. Celia profiles him with piercing accuracy. 'Looking', 'seeing' and 'listening' are repeated words throughout. Celia is the kind of character who gets under people's skin and sizes them up. There is also something chilly and harsh about the way Celia treats Edward as if he were some kind of specimen she is dissecting. Throughout the play Eliot analyses his characters as though they are patients etherized upon a table.

A Day in the Death of Joe Egg
(1967) Peter Nichols

Act 1. The Living-room of Bri and Sheila's house.

Sheila is 'thirty-five, generously built, serious and industrious. When dressed for society she can be captivating'. She and her husband Bri have a ten-year-old spastic daughter – nicknamed Joe Egg by Bri. Caring for Joe tends to dominate their lives; to help cope they have devised an elaborate series of fantasy scenarios and games involving Joe, treating her as if she were only a two-year-old. This helps make their tragic situation bearable. However, the strain of all this is beginning to take its toll on their marriage. Sheila is an ardent member of her local amateur dramatic society and Bri incorrectly insinuates that she is having an affair with Freddie, another member of the society. In this speech the exasperated Sheila confides in the audience.

SHEILA. One of these days I'll hit him. Honestly. (*Brushes hair, looks at audience.*) He thinks because he throws a tantrum I'm going to stay home comforting him and miss the rehearsal and let them all down. He thinks he's only got to cry to get what he wants. I blame his mother. She gave him the kind of suffocating love that makes him think the world revolves around him but because he's too intelligent to believe it really, he gets into these paddies and depressions. And when he's in one of those, he'll do anything to draw attention to himself. That beetle on his face – you saw that. And all this stuff about Freddie. And yet it was Brian made me join these amateurs in the first place, he said I needed to get out more, have a rest from Joe. But she's no trouble. It's Brian. I don't know which is the greatest baby. Watching somebody as limited as Joe over ten years, I've begun to feel she's only one kind of cripple. Everybody's damaged in some way. There's a limit to what we can do. Brian, for instance, he goes so far – and hits the ceiling. Just can't fly any higher. Then he drops to the floor and we get self-pity again . . . despair. I'm sure, though, if he could go farther – he could be a marvellous painter. That's another reason I said I'd join the amateurs: the thought that he'd be forced to go upstairs several nights a week and actually put paint on canvas. And even if he *isn't* any good, he seems to need some work he can be proud of. Something to take his mind off his jealousy of anyone or anything I talk to . . . relatives, friends, pets . . . even pot-plants. I'm sure it's because they take up time he thinks I could be devoting to him. And Joe, most of all, poor love . . . (*She puts brush on table or chair. A thought brings her back.*) Look, you mustn't assume I feel like this in the ordinary way. And even when I *am* a bit down, I shouldn't normally talk about it to a lot of complete strangers. But all this childish temper over Freddie – this showing-off – it's more than I can stand, it makes me boil, honestly! Wouldn't you feel the same? (*Checks her appearance in imaginary full-length glass.*) That's why I'm telling you all this. A lot of total strangers. But wouldn't it make *you* boil? Honestly! A grown man jealous of poor Joe –

COMMENTARY: Peter Nichols' tragicomedy, *A Day in the Death of Joe Egg*, has had a wealth of productions in theatres all over the world and was made into a film in 1972. The play presents a lacerating portrait of a marriage stretched to breaking point by the trauma of having to cope with a spastic child who is dying a little bit more each day. Nichols deals with this difficult subject by balancing rich humour with deep compassion. Actresses like Janet Suzman and Stockard Channing have stamped their own very personal features on the character of Sheila.

This speech opens with an emotional bang that sets the actor in motion. As you may sense this is an exasperated, direct address to the audience. Sheila adopts an easy conversational tone, treating the audience as a friendly confidant. She is letting off steam, venting her frustration. It is more of a complaint and only sometimes a rant. She is a full-blooded, rich creation given to violent and hilarious outbursts. The actress must remember that Sheila is a mother who not only has to care for a special child but also a childish husband. At times the two become confused in her mind and the anger for one is displaced onto the other. Your job here is to convince the audience that what you are saying is just and unselfish. Get them on your side. You can use the hair brushing, indicated in the stage directions, as a physical means of counter-pointing the words. It can become violent or gentle, slow or vigorous. This kind of an emotional outburst, without any false constraints, makes for ideal auditioning material.

East
(1975) Steven Berkoff

Scene 7. A bare stage. Sylv's Longing Speech.

Sylv (18–20) is an East End girl. She is Les's girlfriend.

SYLV. I for once would like to be a fella, unwholesome both in deed and word and lounge around one leg cocked up and car keys tinkling on my pinky. Give a kick* at talent strolling and impale them with an impertinent and fixed stare . . . hand in Levi-Strauss and teeth grinding, and that super unworrisome flesh that toys between your thighs, that we must genuflect and kneel to, that we are beaten across the skull with. Wish I could cruise around and pull those tarts and slags whose hearts would break as he swiftly chews us up and spits us out again . . . the almighty boot! Nay, not fair that those pricks get all the fun – with their big raucous voices and one dozen weekly fucks . . . cave mouths, shout, burp and Guinness-soaked . . . If I dare do that . . . 'What an old scrubber-slag-head' utter their fast and vicious lips . . . so I'd like to be a fella. Strolling down the front with the lads and making minute and limited wars with knife-worn splatter and invective splurge. And not have the emblem of his scummy lust to Persil out with hectic scrub . . . just my Johnny tool to keep from harm and out of mischief . . . my snarling beasty to water and feed from time to rotten time . . . to dip my wick into any old dark and hot with no conscience or love groan . . . doth he possess the plague in gangrened bliss to donate to me and not give a shit. I am

*Give a kick eye up

snarled beneath his bristly glass-edged jaw, beneath a moving sack of leer and hard and be a waste-bin for his excessives and embellishments and ('No . . . no . . . not tonight my friend, a dangerous time is here in case your tadpoles start a forest fire in my oven or even just a bun . . . you won't will you? . . . you will be careful (Yes!) . . . you won't . . . not inside (No!) Not tonight . . . ('Doth thou not love me then') he quests ('nor feel my intense pain, then see me not again, for thou must sacrifice thy altar of lust-pink and pornographia to my tempered, sullen and purple swollen flesh.') Oh Micky! Micky! Wait until tomorrow. ('Tomorrow I may be dead,' he chants in dirge of minor key . . . 'by then my softly flesh may lie in shreds and curling on the streets a victim of nuclear aggro from the powers that deal out death on wholesale scale and liquidise your little Mick to tar, and what was once a silken mass of moving ecstasy programmed by filthy raunchy lust lay now a charred and bitter heap.') Oh who can put it back again those swivel hips/ball-bearing joints flicker spine and tongue like a preying Mantis . . . ('so listen', he adds 'dunk-head and splatter-pull . . . seize the time before time doth seize thee . . . you of the intricate wrist and juice imbiber from the holy North and South.' He sprach . . . 'Give me all now or "it" may with my balls explode, such things are known when passion's smarting angels are defied and I may die in loathsome sickness here upon this plastic and formica divan (Mum and Dad meanwhile in deathly lock of wrath from heavy bingo economic loss . . .') So wrench open, deflower, unpeel, unzip . . . pull off . . . tear round knee tights stuck . . . get your shoes off . . . Ow. Knickers (caught on heel) . . . OOOh, zip hurts . . . dive in and out . . . more a whip in, like a visit – quick, can't stay just sheltering from the rain – cup o'tea hot and fast . . . hot plunge-squirge and sklenge mixed for a brief 'hallo'. A rash of OOhs and Aaaahs quiver and hummmmmmy . . . mmm . . . then hot and flushy he climbs off (come in number 4) and my tears those holy relics

35

of young love tracing mortal paths to Elysium down my cheeks . . . while the 'he' with fag choke and smoke . . . tooth-grin-zip-up . . . me lying looking at the future flashing across the ceiling. He, flashing his comb through his barnet and reddened cheeks blood-soaked (like a saucy cherub, so lovable sometimes you know how boys have this lovely thing about them, some little-boy habit that makes them adorable, crushable-eatable-sweetable-dolly cuddly though sometimes you could kill them) and me lying there a pile of satiate bone and floppy tits flesh-pinched and crackfull of his slop containing God only knows what other infernos but thought I tasted something very strange on his straining dangle which he is wont to offer to me sacrificial like . . . Oh let me be a bloke and sit back curseless, nor forever join the queue of curlered birds outside the loo for dire-emergency . . . do we piss more than men or something . . . nor break my heels in escalators and flash my ass, ascending stairs, to the vile multitude who fantasize me in their quick sex-lustered movies in which I am cast as the queen of slut and yield . . . let me be a bloke and wear trousers stuffed and have pectorals instead of boobs, abdominal and latissimus-dorsi, a web of knotted muscular armature to whip my angered fist into the flesh-pain of sprach-offenders who dare to cast on me their leery cautious minces . . . stab them with fear and have a dozen flesh-hot weekly . . . sleep well and mum fussed, breakfast shoved, 'who's been a naughty boy then', to this pasty wreck of skin and bone gasping in his bed skyving work through riotous folly, bloodlet assault and all night band and 'our lad's a lad, and sown his wild then has he and did you cut yourself a slice' . . . while 'get yourself to the office Sylv or you'll be late,' and the sack in its bed is parlering for another cup of rosy. He's lying in bed whiles I'm on the Underground getting goosed in the rush hour between Mile End and Tottenham Court Road by some creepy arsehole with dandruff, a wife and three accidental kids and who's

36

probably in the accounts department . . . most perverts come from there.

COMMENTARY: *East* is a play that Steven Berkoff wrote as a homage to his youth in London's East End. Within this vibrant, anarchic comedy is a cry of revolt against waste and frustration. It seethes with passion, violence and anger. The lippy language captures the flair of youth argot with its references to hipster fashion, in-spots and in-words. Berkoff's dynamic characters are full of energy but have nowhere to go. They are articulate in their own idiosyncratic ways, but with the quality of whirlwinds spiralling in on themselves.

This is one of the most unusual female speeches in modern drama. It is about gender crossing. Sylv is not a feminist; she is a very feminine and flirtatious East End girl with a mind, and mouth, of her own. The role requires bold, fearless acting and the decision to do a sexy, funky turn on stage. The actor must feel physically free to find the actions the language demands, to mince and strut, to flaunt and flash. However free-form and improvisatory the speech might seem it requires control, precision and planning to make it work effectively. The speech is a wildly satirical take on penis envy and demands imaginative, transformational acting. Enjoy Sylv's wicked and outrageous humour as she relishes all the possibilities and options of being a 'fella'. Steven Berkoff describes the performance style for this speech as follows: 'The acting has to be loose and smacking of danger . . . it must smart and whip out like a fairy's wicked lash. There is no reserve and therefore no embarrassment.' In the language there is 'cross-fertilisation with Shakespeare' with a 'few classical allusions'. Berkoff also indicates the speech can be done most effectively with either an East End (London) or Lower East Side (New York) accent. In other words, this is highly urban speech, full of the syncopated rhythms of the city streets. The sound of the words evokes their sense. It requires good pacing since the monologue is written to sound almost like a song. So watch for the rhythm and style shifts and be prepared to go where the words take you. Like so many of Berkoff's monologues, this one is almost a one-act play in itself.

Faith Healer
(1979) Brian Friel

Part 2. A bare room with a wooden chair and small table.

Grace Hardy, an Englishwoman, is 'in early middle-age. Indifferent to her appearance and barely concealing her distraught mental state. Smoking a lot – sometimes lighting one cigarette from the other'. She is a trained solicitor, but gives up her promising career when she marries Francis (Frank) Hardy, a charismatic Irishman and faith healer. Together they travel around Britain in an old van, moving endlessly from one venue to another with Teddy, Frank's loyal manager. Grace becomes pregnant but her baby is stillborn in a desolate field near Kinlochbervie a Scottish village. Frank abandons Grace, leaving Teddy to look after her. Grace later witnesses the savage murder of her husband in a rural Irish pub. Her mental state has been extremely fragile since then. In this monologue she reminisces about the burial of her baby.

GRACE (*quietly, almost dreamily*). Kinlochbervie's where the baby's buried, two miles south of the village, in a field on the left-hand side of the road as you go north. Funny, isn't it, but I've never met anybody who's been to Kinlochbervie, not even Scottish people. But it *is* a very small village and very remote, right away up in the north of Sutherland, about as far north as you can go in Scotland. And the people there told me that in good weather it is very beautiful and that you can see right across the sea to the Isle of Lewis in the Outer Hebrides. We just happened to be there and we were never back there again and the week that we were there it rained all the time, not really rained but a heavy wet mist so that you could scarcely see across the road. But I'm sure it is a beautiful place in good weather. Anyhow, that's where the

38

baby's buried, in Kinlochbervie, in Sutherland, in the north of Scotland. Frank made a wooden cross to mark the grave and painted it white and wrote across it *Infant Child of Francis and Grace Hardy* – no name, of course, because it was stillborn – just *Infant Child*. And I'm sure that cross is gone by now because it was a fragile thing and there were cows in the field and it wasn't a real cemetery anyway. And I had the baby in the back of the van and there was no nurse or doctor so no one knew anything about it except Frank and Teddy and me. And there was no clergyman at the graveside – Frank just said a few prayers that he made up. So there is no record of any kind. And he never talked about it afterwards; never once mentioned it again; and because he didn't, neither did I. So that was it. Over and done with. A finished thing. Yes. But I think it's a nice name Kinlochbervie – a complete sound – a name you wouldn't forget easily . . .

COMMENTARY: Brian Friel's *Faith Healer* is an incantatory, poetic drama in which three characters tell differing versions of the same tragic events through four interlocking monologues. It is a play about desolation and failure. When acted effectively and truthfully the speeches sound like dreams retold. The exact order of events is always left in doubt. Throughout the play there is no attempt to create a fourth wall, so what the characters say, by way of heartbreaking confession, must be shared openly and intimately with the audience as though they sit in judgement.

Grace, a genteel Englishwoman, is a character at the end of her tether. She is tired and frazzled. She may be in the midst of planning something dire for herself. Her speech is as desolate as her life and captures the feel of a lonely figure somewhere in the midst of an open landscape. The image of a buried child is a potent one for the actor. Yet the whole birth event is described without emotion and in matter-of-fact details. In other words, you have to play this speech against the emotion, avoiding all self-pity. Cancel it out if you can to capture the character's struggle. The stillness in the speech – reinforced by the notion of a stillborn child – gives the memory of the event an almost vanishing quality ('Over and done with. A finished thing'). The actor must remember that Grace cannot forget an unforgettable and regrettable incident. The name 'Kinlochbervie,' an invocation that begins and ends the speech, should provoke deep feelings about the loss of kin and baby. In a later monologue by Teddy, we learn that Grace commits suicide.

The Glass Menagerie
(1945) Tennessee Williams

Scene 1. The Wingfield apartment in St Louis.

Amanda Wingfield (40s) is Tom and Laura's mother. She is a 'little woman of great but confused vitality clinging frantically to another time and place. Her characterization must be carefully created, not copied from type. She is not paranoiac, but her life is paranoia. There is much to admire in Amanda, and as much to love and pity as there is to laugh at. Certainly she has endurance and a kind of heroism, and though her foolishness makes her unwittingly cruel at times, there is tenderness in her slight person'. In this scene she reminisces about her 'gentlemen callers'.

AMANDA. My callers were gentlemen – all! Among my callers were some of the most prominent young planters of the Mississippi Delta – planters and sons of planters! There was young Champ Laughlin who later became vice-president of the Delta Planters Bank. Hadley Stevenson who was drowned in Moon Lake and left his widow one hundred and fifty thousand in Government bonds. There were the Cutrere brothers, Wesley and Bates. Bates was one of my bright particular beaux! He got in a quarrel with that wild Wainwright boy. They shot it out on the floor of Moon Lake Casino. Bates was shot through the stomach. Died in the ambulance on his way to Memphis. His widow was also well provided-for, came into eight or ten thousand acres, that's all. She married him on the rebound – never loved her – carried my picture on him the night he died! And there was that boy that every girl in the Delta had set her cap for! That beautiful, brilliant young Fitzhugh boy from Greene County!

[TOM. What did he leave his widow?]

He never married! Gracious, you talk as though all of my old admirers had turned up their toes to the daisies!

[TOM. Isn't this the first you've mentioned that still survives?]

That Fitzhugh boy went North and made a fortune – came to be known as the Wolf of Wall Street! He had the Midas touch, whatever he touched turned to gold! And I could have been Mrs Duncan J. Fitzhugh, mind you! But – I picked your *father*!

COMMENTARY: Tennessee Williams' *The Glass Menagerie*, with its delicate illusions always on the verge of being shattered, is one of the best-wrought American dramas. The play reveals the past as a potent memory full of dreams and nostalgia, pain and regret. Williams evokes an atmospheric stage world and peoples it with characters who invite compassion and sympathy from the audience. This is Tennessee Williams' most consciously autobiographical play and was his first great success in the theatre.

Amanda is too often played as an old woman although she is only in her forties and still brimming with health and flirtatiousness. Her youth has evaporated only to be recaptured in nostalgic flights of memory like this. The technique used here is similar to the one Williams uses in *A Streetcar Named Desire* – romancing the past – and indeed Amanda seems to be a trial portrait of Blanche DuBois (*see page 133*). Notice all the personal touches that Amanda inserts in her narrative to make it vividly real ('my bright particular beaux', 'carried my picture with him on the night he died'). Reminiscing, for Amanda, is like opening a jewel box filled with glittering memories. Each 'beau' is a precious trinket. How much of this is true is anyone's guess. She has probably told this story so many times that she has perfected its telling and all its 'particular' details. For Amanda the fiction must have a present reality each time she repeats it. The actor must also decide for herself why she is telling this story. Is it to relieve the gloom of her current circumstances? To engage in a bit of daydreaming? Or perhaps even to make her son jealous or her daughter envious? Part of

Amanda's strength as a character comes from the power and control she exerts over her impressionable and emotionally dependent children.

The Good Person of Sichuan

(1939–40) Bertolt Brecht

Scene 4. The Tobacco shop.

Shen Te (20s) is a prostitute in 'the capital of Sichuan, a half-westernized city'. Three gods come to visit the city to find a good person. Shen Te is the only one who qualifies because she offers them a room for the night. With the money they give her she opens a tobacconist shop, but immediately she becomes the victim of parasites who take advantage of her good nature. To meet her growing debts and protect herself against the world, she 'invents' an unscrupulous cousin, Shui Ta, whom she impersonates. As Shen Te she falls in love with an air pilot, Sun, and enlists Shui Ta to arrange her marriage. In this scene Sun demands that Shui Ta sells the shop to raise money for him to pursue his career. Sun boasts that Shen Te is merely a sentimental female in thrall to his masculine charms. Alone, Shui Ta reacts to Sun's bluntness.

SHUI TA. The shop's gone! He doesn't love her! I'm lost! (*He starts pacing about like a caged beast, repeating over and over 'The shop's gone!' until he suddenly stops and addresses* MRS SHIN.) Shin, you grew up in the gutter, and so did I. Are we reckless? No. Are we without the required measure of brutality? No. I'm prepared to grab you by the throat and shake you until you spit out the coin you stole from me, and you know it. The times are vile, this town is hell, but we flatten ourselves against the smooth walls and we climb. Then one of us is overtaken by disaster: he's in love. That's it, he's finished. A moment of weakness, and he's done for. How are we to free ourselves of *every* weakness, especially this most fatal one of all, love? Love is too costly! It's impossible! Then again, tell me, can one live and be forever on one's guard? What kind of world is that?

Caresses turn to strangling.
The sigh of love becomes a cry of fear.
Why are the vultures circling?
There's a woman going to meet her man.

Scene 7. Yard behind Shen Te's Tobacco shop.

During the wedding ceremony, Sun rejects Shen Te because she favours settling her debts instead of giving him her money. Here she is alone and pregnant.

SHEN TE (*she looks at her belly, touches it and a great joy appears on her face. Quietly*). Oh joy! There is a small person being born inside me. You can't see anything yet. But I know he's there. The world is waiting for him, secretly. In the cities they are saying: there is a man coming who will be someone to reckon with. (*She presents her little son to the audience.*)
An airman!
Greet the new conqueror
Of uncharted regions and inaccessible mountain chains.
    A man
Who carries the mail over inhospitable deserts
From one person to another!
(*She starts walking to and fro, leading her son by the hand.*)
Come, my son. Take a look at the world. This here is a tree. Bow and greet it. (*She shows him how.*) There, now you're acquainted. Stop, here comes the water-seller. He is a friend, you may shake his hand. Don't be afraid! A glass of fresh water for my son. It's a warm day. (*She gives him the glass.*) Uh oh, the policeman! We'll avoid him. Perhaps we'll treat ourselves to a few cherries from the garden of the rich

45

Mr Feh Pung. But we mustn't let him see us! Come on, little fatherless one! You want cherries just the same! Quietly, son, quietly! (*They go on tiptoe, circumspectly.*) No, this way, we can hide behind that bush. No, it's a mistake to go straight up to it, in this case. (*He appears to be pulling her one way, she to resist.*) We must be sensible. (*Suddenly she gives in.*) All right, if you want to head directly for it . . . (*She lifts him up.*) Can you reach the cherries? Stuff them in your mouth, that's the best hiding place for them. (*She eats one herself, which he puts in her mouth.*) Mmm, sweet. Drat it, here's the policeman. Now we have to run. (*They flee.*) There's the street. Easy now, just walk along normally, so we don't catch his eye. As if nothing had happened at all . . . (*She sings, strolling with the child.*)

A plum fell out of the sky
And attacked a passer-by.
The fellow stopped
And watched it drop
And into his mouth it popped.

Scene 8. Courtroom.

Shui Ta is brought to trial for the murder of his other half Shen Te. The three gods sit in judgement. Shui Ta asks for the court to be cleared and then, stripping off the disguise of Shui Ta, Shen Te begins her confession.

SHEN TE. Yes, it's me, I am Shui Ta and Shen Te.
Your instruction once given me
To be good and to live
Ripped me in two like a lightning bolt.
I don't know how it came about. I could not be
46

Good to others and at the same time to myself,
To help others and myself was beyond me.
Oh, your world is so difficult!
Too much hardship, too much despair.
Hold out a hand to help,
And it will be torn off! Aid the straggler,
And you yourself are lost! Who could long refrain
From becoming evil, where dog eats dog?
From where was I to draw all that was needed?
Only out of myself! But that finished me off!
The weight of good intentions
Crushed me. But when I did ill,
Then I went around in pomp, and ate the best meat.
Something must be wrong with your world.
And why is there a reward for wrongdoing,
And why do such harsh punishments
Await the good? Oh, I felt such a desire
To spoil myself! And there was a secret
Wisdom in me, because my foster-mother
Washed me in gutter water. That
Sharpened my eye. But pity
So hurt me, that I fell into a savage temper
At the sight of misery. Then
I felt myself changing, and
My lips becoming hard. The kind word
Tasted as ashes in my mouth. And yet
I wanted to be an angel in the suburbs.
To give was bliss to me. A happy face,
And I walked on air.
Condemn me: all I did
I did to help my neighbour.
To love the man I loved, and
To save my little son from poverty.
For your great plan, O gods,
I was human and too small.

Translation by Michael Hofmann

COMMENTARY: Brecht's great parable about the division between goodness and necessity found an ideal metaphor in the actor: Shen Te (the prostitute with the heart of gold) and Shui Ta (a hardened streetwise merchant) are meant to be played by the same woman. The play lives or dies on the merits of the central performance. It has attracted such great performers as Janet Suzman and Fiona Shaw. In playing the part(s) the actor must use different sides of herself: show emotion and then keep it violently under wraps. The dramatist helps in this challenge by patterning the characters' speeches in different ways: blunt prose, excessive lyricism, song, proverbial sayings and poems. Emotion is either released or kept hidden. We've included several speeches from the play so that the performer can test her skill against Brecht's design and discover for herself the needs imbedded in this ever-changing role.

In the first speech Shui Ta comes across as blunt and direct. The feminine side of the character does come through, in phrases such as 'He doesn't love her!', but male practicality quickly stifles any emotional gesture. The objective here is to capture Shui Ta's brutal, anti-romantic stance. He is very rooted to the earth. In the second speech Shen Te's flight of fancy, her unfettered happiness about the life growing inside her, shows a completely different aspect of the character. Her feelings of joy take flight. She uses her physicality in a completely different way. We see a mother enjoying, cautioning and protecting an imaginary child. But in the world of this play evil is never far away and innocence needs protection. In the final speech both sides of the character merge. 'She' and 'He' must show both sides of self simultaneously. It also gives the actor a keen insight into the play's meaning. Goodness *and* evil are alternately masked. We show one side and then another, as we wrestle with moral dilemmas. The speech captures the very essence of what it is to be human and humane. The actor might also try doing these speeches employing masks. Ultimately, however, the actor's own face should replace the effects of the mask.

Happy Days
(1961) Samuel Beckett

Act 1. Expanse of scorched grass rising to a low mound. Blazing light.

Winnie (50s) is 'imbedded up to above her waist in exact centre of mound.' She is 'well preserved, blonde for preference, plump, arms and shoulders bare, low bodice, big bosom, pearl necklet. . . . Beside her on ground to her left a capacious black bag, shopping variety, and to her right a collapsible parasol. . . . To her right and rear, lying asleep on ground, hidden by mound, Willie'.

WINNIE (*gazing at zenith*). Another heavenly day. (*Pause. Head back level, eyes front, pause. She clasps hands to breast, closes eyes. Lips move in inaudible prayer, say ten seconds. Lips still. Hands remain clasped. Low.*) For Jesus Christ sake Amen. (*Eyes open, hands unclasp, return to mound. Pause. She clasps hands to breast again, closes eyes, lips move again in inaudible addendum, say five seconds. Low.*) World without end Amen. (*Eyes open, hands unclasp, return to mound. Pause.*) Begin, Winnie. (*Pause.*) Begin your day, Winnie. (*Pause. She turns to bag, rummages in it without moving it from its place, brings out toothbrush, rummages again, brings out flat tube of toothpaste, turns back front, unscrews cap of tube, lays cap on ground, squeezes with difficulty small blob of paste on brush, holds tube in one hand and brushes teeth with other. She turns modestly aside and back to her right to spit out behind mound. In this position her eyes rest on* WILLIE. *She spits out. She cranes a little further back and down. Loud.*) Hoo-oo! (*Pause. Louder.*) Hoo-oo! (*Pause. Tender smile as she turns back front, lays down brush.*) Poor Willie – (*examines tube,*

49

smile off) – running out – (*looks for cap*) – ah well – (*finds cap*) – can't be helped – (*screws cap on*) – just one of those old things – (*lays down tube*) – another of those old things – (*turns towards bag*) – just can't be cured – (*rummages in bag*) – cannot be cured – (*brings out small mirror, turns back front*) – ah yes – (*inspects teeth in mirror*) – poor dear Willie – (*testing upper front teeth with thumb, indistinctly*) – good Lord! – (*pulling back upper lip to inspect gums, do.*) – good God! – (*pulling back corner of mouth, mouth open, do.*) – ah well – (*other corner, do.*) – no worse – (*abandons inspection, normal speech*) – no better, no worse – (*lays down mirror*) – no change – (*wipes fingers on grass*) – no pain – (*looks for toothbrush*) – hardly any – (*takes up toothbrush*) – great thing that – (*examines handle of brush*) – nothing like it – (*examines handle, reads*) – pure . . . what? – (*pause*) – what? – (*lays down brush*) – ah yes – (*turns towards bag*) – poor Willie – (*rummages in bag*) – no zest – (*rummages*) – for anything – (*brings out spectacles in case*) – no interest – (*turns back front*) – in life – (*takes spectacles from case*) – poor dear Willie – (*lays down case*) – sleep for ever – (*opens spectacles*) – marvellous gift – (*puts on spectacles*) – nothing to touch it – (*looks for toothbrush*) – in my opinion – (*takes up toothbrush*) – always said so – (*examines handle of brush*) – wish I had it – (*examines handle, reads*) – genuine . . . pure . . . what? – (*lays down brush*) – blind next – (*takes off spectacles*) – ah well – (*lays down spectacles*) – seen enough – (*feels in bodice for handkerchief*) – I suppose – (*takes out folded handkerchief*) – by now – (*shakes out handkerchief*) – what are those wonderful lines – (*wipes one eye*) – woe woe is me – (*wipes the other*) – to see what I see – (*looks for spectacles*) – ah yes – (*takes up spectacles*) – wouldn't miss it – (*starts polishing spectacles, breathing on lenses*) – or would I? – (*polishes*) – holy light – (*polishes*) – holy light – (*polishes*) – bob up out of dark – (*polishes*) – blaze of hellish light. (*Stops polishing, raises face to sky, pause, head back level, resumes polishing, stops polishing, cranes back to her right and down.*) Hoo-oo! (*Pause. Tender smile as she turns*

50

back front and resumes polishing. Smile off.) Marvellous gift –
(*stops polishing, lays down spectacles*) – wish I had it – (*folds handkerchief*) – ah well – (*puts handkerchief back in bodice*) – can't complain – (*looks for spectacles*) – no no – (*takes up spectacles*) – mustn't complain – (*holds up spectacles, looks through lens*) – so much to be thankful for – (*looks through other lens*) – no pain – (*puts on spectacles*) – hardly any – (*looks for toothbrush*) – wonderful thing that – (*takes up toothbrush*) – nothing like it – (*examines handle of brush*) – slight headache sometimes – (*examines handle, reads*) – guaranteed . . . genuine . . . pure . . . what? – (*looks closer*) – genuine pure . . . – (*takes handkerchief from bodice*) – ah yes – (*shakes out handkerchief*) – occasional mild migraine – (*starts wiping handle of brush*) – it comes – (*wipes*) – then goes – (*wiping mechanically*) – ah yes – (*wiping*) – many mercies – (*wiping*) – great mercies – (*stops wiping, fixed lost gaze, brokenly*) – prayers perhaps not for naught – (*pause, do.*) – first thing – (*pause, do.*) – last thing – (*head down, resumes wiping, stops wiping, head up, calmed, wipes eyes, folds handkerchief, puts it back in bodice, examines handle of brush, reads*) – fully guaranteed . . . genuine pure . . . – (*looks closer*) – genuine pure . . . (*Takes off spectacles, lays them and brush down, gazes before her.*) Old things. (*Pause.*) Old Eyes. (*Long pause.*) On, Winnie.

COMMENTARY: Beckett's *Happy Days* is a comedy of desperation that explores the very nature of daily existence. The drama reveals human nature reduced to its bare essentials, struggling to preserve itself. Imprisoned and immobile in their respective mounds, Winnie, and to a lesser extent Willie, enact the rituals of survival. As the minutiae of daily life take on epic proportions, Winnie struggles to give her life definition, meaning and form. In Winnie, Beckett created a role that demands virtuoso acting. She has been played by such extraordinary actresses as Madeleine Rénaud (who created Winnie in Paris), Ruth White, Peggy Ashcroft and Billie

Whitelaw. Every actress who plays Winnie has to invent her for herself.

From her first words ('Another heavenly day') Winnie reveals her innate optimism. Each and every day Winnie embarks on the same tasks – saying prayers, brushing teeth, combing hair, polishing spectacles, etc. Winnie is a creature of daily routine and habits, each of which help her renew and reaffirm her identity. There is a precision in this routine ritual. Winnie is exactly like a stage actress who has to repeat the same lines and business night after night. She needs an audience to give her performance meaning and guarantee her existence; she performs for Willie on-stage and the audience in the theatre. Life, for the characters in all of Beckett's dramas, takes on the quality of a performance in a long-running play. He exposes the mundanity that can pile up like a mound of earth, creating a living grave. Language and performance are paired and syncopated throughout the speech: Winnie speaks carefully chosen words and then executes a meticulous action. The actress should pay particular attention to the activities Winnie describes in this speech. An elaborate toilette is being carried out under the blazing sun. Notice her relationship to all the treasured contents of her handbag; they almost have personalities. Winnie and her husband Willie seem to be old age pensioners out for a day at the seaside. They are also like sand crabs doing the routines that will help them to survive. To play Winnie best you have to get past her vanity and locate the survivor inside the character. Words define her existence and her actions reinforce them; she speaks and acts and therefore she is.

Hello and Goodbye
(1965) Athol Fugard

Act 1. A kitchen table and four chairs, lit by a solitary electric light hanging above. Port Elizabeth, South Africa.

Hester Smit (34) is a prostitute in Johannesburg. She returns home to visit her father and younger brother Johnnie. She has been gone for twelve years, driven away by hate. The letter she sends informing them of her arrival never arrives so her return is a surprise. In this early scene she encounters Johnnie who says he doesn't recognise her. His hostility and suspicion force her to prove her identity. As she says, she is 'passing through. It's hello and goodbye'. In this speech she describes her journey back home.

HESTER. To hell with what I said. I'm here (*Looking around.*) Mind you it's easier than I thought.
[JOHNNIE. I've noticed that. It's always easier than we think.]
I thought it would be hard, or hurt – something like that. But here I am and it isn't so bad.
[JOHNNIE. It's never so bad as we think.]
Do you know what I'm talking about.
[JOHNNIE. No.]
Then shut up and listen! (*Pause.*) I'm talking about coming back. You see I tried hell of a hard to remember. That was a mistake. I got frightened.
[JOHNNIE. Of what?]
Not like that. Maybe frightened is wrong. Don't get any ideas I'm scared of you lot. Just because I come back doesn't mean I'm hard up. But at Kommodagga there was a long stop – I started remembering and that made me . . . (*Groping for words.*) . . . I think nerves is better. The whole

53

business was getting on my nerves! The heat, sitting there sweating and waiting! I'm not one for waiting. It was the slow train, you see. All stops. And then also this old bitch in the compartment. I hate them when they're like that – fat and dressed in black like Bibles because somebody's dead, and calling me Ou★ Sister. I had her from Nooupoort and it was non-stop all the time about the Kingdom of Heaven was at hand and swimming on Sunday and all that rubbish. Because I was remembering, you see! It wasn't that I couldn't. I could. It was seeing it again that worried me. The same. Do you understand? Coming back and seeing it all still the same. I wasn't frightened of there being changes. I said to myself, I hope there is changes. Please let it be different and strange, even if I get lost and got to ask my way. I won't mind. But to think of it all still the same, the way it was, and me coming back to find it like that . . . ! Sick! It made me sick on the stomach. There was fruit cake with the afternoon tea and I almost vomited. And every time just when I'm ready to be brave Ou Sister starts again on the Kingdom and Jesus doesn't like lipstick. By then I had her in a big way. So when she asks me if I seen the light I said no because I preferred the dark! Just like that, and I went outside to stand in the gangway. But next stop I see it's still only Boesmanspoort and ninety miles to go so it all starts again. Only it's worse now, because I start remembering like never before. Those windy days with nothing to do; the dust in the street! Even the colour of things – so clear, man, it could have been yesterday. The way the grass went grey around the laundry drain on the other side, the foam in the river, and inside those Indian women ironing white shirts. And the smell, that special ironing smell – warm and damp – with them talking funny Indian and looking sad. Smells! I could give you smells a mile long – backyard smells, Sunday smells, and what about the Chinaman shop on the corner! Is he still

★**Ou** old

54

there? That did it. Don't ask me why – something to do with no pennies for sweets – but that did it. If it's still there I said, if there's still those sacks of beans and sugar and rice on the floor with everything smelling that special way when I walk past, I'll bring up on the spot like a dog, so help me God. So then I said, No, this isn't wise. Get off at Coega and catch the next one back to Jo'burg. Send them a telegram, even if it's a lie – sick of something, which was almost true. I was ready to do it. 'Strue's God! But the next stop was Sandflats and there suddenly I see it's sunset. Somebody in the gangway said we were two hours late and it will be dark when we get in. That will help me, won't it, I think to myself. And it did. Because it was – dark and me feeling like a stranger in the taxi. All my life I been noticing this, the way night works, the way it makes you feel home is somewhere else. Even with the lights on, like now, looking at this . . . I don't know. It is and it isn't. I'm not certain. It could be true. Tomorrow will tell. I never have doubts in daylight. So that was Jo'burg to P. E. second class. Over to you.

COMMENTARY: In *Hello and Goodbye* Athol Fugard explores the relationship between two poor white Afrikaners, a brother and sister, with hatred in their blood. In each of his plays Fugard creates a vivid theatrical portrait of the South African town in which he grew up. He portrays characters who are lonely, dispossessed wanderers. Home and homeland are vague locations to them. Yet they still feel rooted, and, despite themselves, especially rooted to other people.

Fugard's best dramas centre on a confrontation. Here it is between Hester and Johnnie, between the words hello and goodbye. Going and coming are the two simple yet complex actions described again and again throughout the speeches and scenes of this play. The actress must take us through Hester's journey home: not just any journey, but a long, hot, dusty train trip through a bleak landscape. Ultimately the journey is literally taking her back to a past she would like to forget. She is practically dragging herself home against her will, as though ineluctably drawn there. Notice how angry and resentful she is about everyone and everything she encounters. Hester seems to be the kind of person always spoiling for a fight. The monologue is in monochrome; everything she sees is black and white, right and wrong. Her words and descriptions are vivid and clipped. The journey back has been full of unpleasant smells and sensations, of restless irritations and annoying encounters. She hasn't slept. After such a trip and an indifferent welcome home is it any wonder that Hester is exhausted and testy?

The House of Blue Leaves

(1971) John Guare

Act 1. A shabby apartment in Sunnyside, Queens (New York). A living room filled with many lamps and pictures of movie stars and jungle animals. 4.45 a.m. on October 4th, 1965.

Bunny Flingus (39) 'is a pretty, pink, electric woman . . . She wears a fur-collar coat and plastic booties, and two Brownie cameras on strings clunking against a pair of binoculars. At the moment she is freezing, uncomfortable and furious.' She is Artie Shaughnessy's mistress. She has been out all night in the cold waiting to witness an historic event: the Pope's arrival in New York. She has just returned and wakes Artie who is asleep on the sofa in his sleeping bag. This speech opens the play.

BUNNY. You know what your trouble is? You got no sense of history. You know that? Are you aware of that? Lock yourself up against history, get drowned by the whole tide of human events. Sleep it away in your bed. Your bag. Zip yourself in, Artie. The greatest tide in the history of the world is coming in today, so don't get your feet wet.
[ARTIE (*picking up his glow-in-the-dark alarm*). It's quarter to five in the morning, Bunny –]
Lucky for you I got a sense of history. (*Sits on the edge of the couch. Picks up the newspaper on the floor.*) You finished last night's? Oooo. It's freezing out there. Breath's coming out of everybody's mouth like a balloon in a cartoon. (*Rips the paper into long shreds and stuffs it down into the plastic booties she wears.*) People have been up for hours. Queens Boulevard – lined for blocks already! Steam coming out of everybody's mouth! Cripples laid out in the street in stretchers with earmuffs on over their bandages. Nuns – you never seen so many nuns in your life! Ordinary people like

57

you and me in from New Jersey and Connecticut and there's a lady even drove in from Ohio – Ohio! – just for today! She drove four of the most crippled people in Toledo. They're stretched out in the gutter waiting for the sun to come out so they can start snapping pictures. I haven't seen so many people, Artie, so excited since the première of *Cleopatra*. It's that big. Breathe! There's miracles in the air!

[ARTIE. It's soot, Bunny. Polluted air.]

All these out-of-staters driving in with cameras and thermos bottles and you live right here and you're all zipped in like a turtle. Miss Henshaw, the old lady who's the check-out girl at A&P who gyps everybody – her nephew is a cop and she's saving us two divine places right by the curb. You're not the only one with connections. But she can't save them forever. Oh God, Artie, what a morning! You should see the stars!!! I know all the stars from the time I worked for that astronomer and you should see Orion – O'Ryan: the Irish constellation – I haven't looked up and seen stars in years! I held my autograph book up and let Jupiter shine on it. Jupiter and Venus and Mars. They're all out! You got to come see Orion. He's the hunter and he's pulling his arrow back so tight in the sky like a Connect-the-Dots picture made up of all these burning planets. If he ever lets that arrow go, he'll shoot all the other stars out of the sky – what a welcome for the Pope! And right now, the Pope is flying through the star-filled sky, bumping planets out of the way, and he's asleep dreaming of the mobs waiting for him. When famous people go to sleep at night, it's us they dream of, Artie. The famous ones – they're the real people. We're the creatures of their dreams. You're the dream. I'm the dream. We have to be there for the Pope's dream. Look at the light on the Empire State Building swirling around and around like a burglar's torch looking all through the sky – Everybody's waiting, Artie – everybody!

COMMENTARY: John Guare's *House of Blue Leaves* is a surreal tragicomedy about a family of lost dreamers adrift in a world of topsy-turvy values. The play mixes the Kaufman and Hart tradition of American stage comedy with a drama of modern psychological angst. Its brilliant evocation of stand-up comedy, vaudevillian slapstick and troubled states of mind make it an acting *tour de force*. The mood of the acting changes constantly. Guare has created some of the most memorable oddball characters in modern American drama. On the surface they appear to be cartoons. Underneath, however, they reveal needs and desires as significant as any tragic hero or heroine of classical drama.

Bunny is addicted to fame. She wants to be an eyewitness to history and has been up all night waiting for the main event: the visit of the Pope. Artie is her opposite in every way. She's out and about while he stays cocooned inside a sleeping bag. Bunny not only has a sense of event and history, she has a celestial point of view. As a writer John Guare aims always to release his characters into a higher orbit. He is never content to leave them earthbound for too long. He'd rather see and hear them soar. As soon as Bunny begins to talk about the stars you know she has launched herself aloft. She is practically twitching with excitement. This is both figuratively and literally an upbeat speech; its trajectory rises and rises until it encompasses the whole world: 'Everybody's waiting, Artie – everybody!' Bunny's exasperation and anticipation come in equal measure. She is swept away by all the show-biz glitz and high on the excitement from the mounting crowds. There is offbeat poetry and passion in her busy babbling.

Huis Clos [In Camera/No Exit]
(1944) Jean-Paul Sartre

One act. A drawing-room in Second Empire style.

Inez Serrano (30s), a former post office clerk and a proclaimed lesbian, has recently died. A valet brings her into an elegant, brightly illuminated room with neither mirrors nor windows. Here she is condemned to spend the rest of eternity with two other recently deceased characters: Estelle an attractive socialite and Garcin a weak womanizer. A bizarre triangular relationship develops between them: Inez is interested in Estelle; Estelle is more interested in Garcin; Garcin is most interested in himself. It is Inez who first realizes that they have been brought together to serve as one another's eternal torturers: in this hell there will be no physical torments, there will just be the three of them – forever together. Inez turns on Garcin in this speech when he suggests their best option is studiously to forget that the others are in the room.

INEZ. To forget about the others? How utterly absurd! I *feel* you there, in every pore. Your silence clamours in my ears. You can nail up your mouth, cut your tongue out – but you can't prevent your *being* there. Can you stop your thoughts? I hear them ticking away like a clock, tick-tock, tick-tock, and I'm certain you hear mine. It's all very well skulking on your sofa, but you're everywhere, and every sound comes to me soiled, because you've intercepted it on its way. Why, you've even stolen my face; you know it and I don't! And what about her, about Estelle? You've stolen her from me, too; if she and I were alone do you suppose she'd treat me as she does? No, take your hands from your face. I won't leave you in peace – that would suit your book too well. You'd go on sitting there in a sort of trance, like a yogi, and even if I didn't see her I'd feel it in my bones – that she was making every sound, even the rustle of her dress, for your benefit, throwing you smiles you didn't see. . . . Well, I won't stand for that, I prefer to choose my hell; I prefer to look you in the eyes and fight it out face to face.

Translation by Stuart Gilbert

COMMENTARY: Sartre's *Huis Clos* revolves around the tightly woven dissension among the three characters. They are trapped with their passions and desires in eternal conflict. In Garcin's words, 'Hell is other people'. Even when the characters describe irrelevant details, each story and image comes inexorably back to that main point: human misery is occasioned by other people. In death identities are fixed and the past is a closed book with no hope of retribution. Hell offers only the opportunity to reflect on missed opportunities; there is no longer any choice. Each character has an equal share in this claustrophobic, locked-room drama. At any given moment one or the other is the play's centre.

The game being played here is a sexual one. The trio of characters is in such close proximity – hostages really – that Inez can hear the tick-tock of Garcin's mind. He is driving her crazy. His physical presence revolts her because it denies her the hope that Estelle will ever be interested in her. Everything she says is in close-up and the acting needs magnification as well. The tick-tock is also like a time bomb waiting to explode. This speech is loaded with explosive tension and vindictive rage as Inez launches her verbal attack on Garcin. Language is the only weapon and defence that Sartre allows his characters. The only place he can hide is behind his hands. She even denies him that comfort. Each of the characters is vain and selfish but Inez seems even more spiteful and vicious than the others. Her hatred of men is particularly withering and it is this fact that fuels her anger. Inez concludes on a triumphant note as she delights in the prospect of eternally tormenting Garcin by *her* presence and *her* gaze.

Icarus's Mother
(1965) Sam Shepard

One act. A grassy picnic area near a beach.

Jill (20s) is celebrating July 4th with her girlfriend Pat and three men friends. They have come to the beach for a barbecue. A plane passes overhead and they all watch it making patterns in the sky. When Pat expresses a need 'to pee' she and Jill go off together along the beach. In this scene they return laughing to tell the men of their adventures.

JILL. Do you know – do you know what this idiot did? Do you know what she did! She – we're walking up the beach, see – we're walking along like this. (*She walks very slowly with her head down.*) Very slowly and dejected and sad. So suddenly she stops. We both stop and she says, guess what? And I said what? She says I really do – I really do have to pee after all. (*They both break up.*) So I said all right. I'm very serious with her, see. I say all right, Patsy dear, if you have to you have to. So then she said I have to pee so bad I can't even wait. I have to go right now. Right this very minute. So we're in the middle of the beach with nothing around but sand. No bushes or nothing. So she whips down her pants and crouches right there in the middle of the beach very seriously. And I'm standing there looking around. Sort of standing guard. And do you know what happens? (*They crack up.*) All of a sudden I have to pee too. I mean really bad like she has to. So I whip my pants down and crouch down right beside her. There we are sitting side by side on the beach together. (*She crouches down in the position.*) Like a couple of desert nomads or something. So. You know how it is when you have to pee so bad that you can't pee at all?
62

(BILL *and* HOWARD *nod their heads.*) Well that's what happened. Neither one of us could get anything out and we were straining and groaning and along comes our friend in the jet plane. Except this time he's very low. Right above our heads. Zoom! So there we were. We couldn't stand up because then he'd really see us. And we couldn't run because there was nowhere to run to. So we just sat and pretended we were playing with shells or something. But he kept it up. He kept flying back and forth right above our heads. So do you know what this nut does? (HOWARD *and* BILL *shake their heads.*) She starts waving to him and throwing kisses. Then he really went nuts. He started doing flips and slides with that jet like you've never seen before. (*She stands with her arms outstretched like a plane.*) He went way up and then dropped like a seagull or something. We thought he was going to crash even. Then I started waving and the guy went insane. He flew that thing upside down and backwards and every way you could imagine. And we were cracking up all over the place. We started rolling in the sand and showing him our legs. Then we did some of those nasty dances like they do in bars. Then we both went nuts or something and we took off our pants and ran straight into the water yelling and screaming and waving at his plane.

COMMENTARY: Shepard's *Icarus's Mother* can be seen as a contemporary parable depicting the fall from grace and innocence. The twenty-two-year-old Shepard wrote this play in the midst of the 60s youth culture explosion. His work teems with energy and inventiveness, testing the barriers beyond which on-stage dialogue could be taken. Shepard purposely creates ambiguous and unpredictable characters, offering little background biography and few indications of motivation. From moment to moment in the drama the characters are questing in search of an identity, a sense of self. Each word they speak is an attempt, no matter how apparently inarticulate, at self-definition.

For Shepard the names of his characters always have a sly significance (*see 'La Turista' page 70*) and here Jill is no longer the sweet innocent of the 'Jack and Jill' books. This Jill is a candid and knowing young woman who acts like an embattled commando, seeking protection from an aircraft strafing the beach. The monologue so vividly and literally captures the sense of someone with her pants down, exposed and with nowhere to hide. Her language is simple, realistically idiomatic and down-to-earth. Notice how the short and fractured rhythms propel the pace of her narrative. The actor must convey confusion and even panic along with Jill's sense of hilarity and hysteria. This is an excellent audition speech because it is such a self-contained story. Jill is performing for her on-stage audience, leaving nothing to their imagination. She seems to enjoy being the centre of attention and uses Pat as her silent comic stooge. Notice, too, that as her rapport with her listeners grows so does her confidence and audacity. The actor should decide how far to physicalize the story. Since Shepard gives few clues about the characters, you are never sure who Jill is, where she comes from or what her relationship is to the other characters in the play. Jill seems to make herself up as she goes along. You really need to know nothing at all about Jill. To make the speech really effective just find a part of her inside yourself.

The Iceman Cometh

(1940) Eugene O'Neill

Act 1. The back room bar of Harry Hope's saloon on an early morning in summer, 1912.

Cora (early 20s) is a streetwalker. She 'is a thin peroxide blonde . . . her round face showing the wear and tear of her trade, but still with traces of a doll-like prettiness'. She wears 'the usual tawdry get-up'. She has just come into the saloon and regales the regulars with tales of her previous night's activities.

CORA. No, dis round's on me. I run into luck. Dat's why I dragged Chuck outa bed to celebrate. It was a sailor. I rolled him. (*She giggles.*) Listen, it was a scream. I've run into some nutty souses, but dis guy was de nuttiest. De booze dey dish out around de Brooklyn Navy Yard must be as turrible bug-juice as Harry's. My dogs was givin' out when I seen dis guy holdin' up a lamp-post, so I hurried to get him before a cop did. I says, 'Hello, handsome, wanta have a good time?' Jees, he was paralysed! One of dem polite jags. He tries to bow to me imagine, and I had to prop him up or he'd fell on his nose. And what d'yuh tink he said? 'Lady,' he says, 'can yuh kindly tell me de nearest way to de Museum of Natural History?' (*They all laugh.*) Can yuh imagine! At 2 am. As if I'd know where de dump was anyway. But I says, 'Sure ting, Honey Boy, I'll be only too glad'. So I steered him into a side street where it was dark and propped him against a wall and give him a frisk. (*She giggles.*) And what d'yuh tink he does? Jees, I ain't lyin', he begins to laugh, de big sap! He says, 'Quit ticklin' me'. While I was friskin' him for his roll! I near died! Den I toined him 'round and give him a push to start him. 'Just keep goin',' I told him. 'It's a big white building on your right. You can't miss it.' He must be swimmin' in de North River yet! . . . I picked twelve bucks offa him. Come on, Rocky, set 'em up.

COMMENTARY: O'Neill's *The Iceman Cometh* examines a colourful group of dissolute drunks and assorted hangers-on who inhabit a sleazy New York bar attached to Harry Hope's rooming house. This drama helped to set the style for a range of American genre plays about dreams and disillusion. These include William Saroyan's *The Time of Your Life* and more recent perennials like Robert Patrick's *Kennedy's Children* and Lanford Wilson's *Balm in Gilead* and *Hot l Baltimore*. The free-flowing liquor leads inevitably to free-flowing talk; the bar-room becomes akin to a secular confessional. As the drama progresses each character has a chance to speak out, to articulate his and her hopes and dreams.

Cora is the stereotypical prostitute. Her speech is a triumphant boast as she regales the regulars with the story of her lucky night. Her colloquial speech is full of rich, rounded vowels and is pitched to sound theatrical. Notice the way she uses knowing asides to keep their attention: 'And what do you tink he said?'; 'Can you imagine!'. She is giving an impromptu performance, and she knows how to time her delivery. She easily captivates her audience with her streetwise humour, although they have probably heard her deliver similar tales of rich pickings. Notice what hilarity she finds in misfortune. She is a gold-digger who's struck treasure in the form of 'twelve bucks'. This is a world in which twelve bucks are a small fortune. For Cora, finding such easy money probably is a dream come true.

Jumpers
(1972) Tom Stoppard

Act 1. An elegant, feminine and expensive bedroom

Dotty (25–30) is a 'prematurely-retired musical-comedy actress of some renown'. She is married to George, her former professor and an expert in Moral Philosophy. She is 'very beautiful indeed' and describes herself as 'the incomparable, unreliable and neurotic Dorothy Moore'. Her repertoire as a singer included songs with 'moon' in the title; such as 'Shine on, shine on harvest moon' and 'Blue Moon'. As Dotty stares at the historic moon-landing on her TV she begins a speech which reveals her moonstruck reasons for retiring from the stage.

DOTTY. Poor moon man, falling home like Lucifer. (*She turns off the TV: screen goes white.*) . . . Of course, to somebody *on* it, the moon is always full, so the local idea of a sane action may well differ from ours. (*Pause; stonily*) When they first landed, it was as though I'd seen a unicorn on the television news. . . . It was very interesting, of course. But it certainly spoiled unicorns. (*Pause.*) I tried to explain it to the analyst when everybody in sight was asking me what was the matter. . . . 'What's the matter, darling?' . . . 'What *happened*, baby?' What could I say? I came over funny at work so I went home early. It must happen often enough to a working girl. And why must the damned show go on anyway? So it stopped right then and there, and in a way my retirement was the greatest triumph of my career. Because nobody left.
[GEORGE (*to himself.*) Sam Clegthorpe!]
For nearly an hour they all sat out front, staring at that stupid spangled moon, and they weren't waiting for their money's worth, they were waiting for *news. Is she all right?*

. . . Oh yes, not bad for a bored housewife, eh? – not at all bad for a one-time student amateur bored with keeping house for her professor. And they're still waiting! – my retirement is now almost as long as my career, but they're waiting for me to come back out, and finish my song. And writing me love letters in the meantime. That's right, *not* so bloody bad for a second-class honours with a half-good voice and a certain variety of shakes. It's no good, though. They thought it was overwork or alcohol, but it was just those little grey men in goldfish bowls, clumping about in their lead boots on the television news; it was very interesting, but it certainly spoiled that Juney old moon; and much else besides. . . . The analyst went barking up the wrong tree, of course; I should never have mentioned unicorns to a Freudian.

COMMENTARY: Tom Stoppard's *Jumpers* is an exuberant philosophical farce which literally 'jumps' from place to place, character to character and theme to theme. It wittily defies gravity or any easy categorizing as it bounces around such diverse subjects as science, philosophy, lunar landings, romance, relationships, gymnastics and murder. There is an effervescent quality to Stoppard's dazzlingly agile dialogue which perfectly complements his themes. This modern mystery play is a linguistic, theatrical and philosophical *tour de force*.

Dotty is obsessed by the moon to the point of being loony. She is vivacious and vulnerable, with an almost childlike quality. Dotty, who has a second class degree in Moral Philosophy, speaks in fragments that have their own kind of logic. Notice the clipped and witty style she adopts as she addresses her audience. Although an incurable romantic, Dotty is wise to the nagging problem that once you have men making footprints on the face of the moon modern romance can only be in doubt. She intuitively feels the need to believe in any ideal that could validate her own existence. The innocence that allowed her to sing songs about the moon has been destroyed by a lunar landing. Now she is lost. She dispassionately describes the moment when she 'came over funny' and her 'retirement' from the stage. She suffered what amounts to a crisis of faith. The actor should remember that Dotty is always the consummate performer, delighting in sophisticated whimsy and fancy. She flirts with philosophy as she flirted with her audiences. Her successful cabaret career broke down *in medias res*. She has never quite recovered from the shock of science's triumph over fantasy.

La Turista

(1967) Sam Shepard

Act 1. A hotel room in Mexico.

Salem (20s) and Kent are a young American couple on holiday in Mexico. As the play opens they are in their beds suffering from painful sunburn. Kent also has diarrhoea; the 'la turista' of the title. A native boy enters their room while they are still in bed. In response to his silence they offer him handfuls of money from their suitcase, which he ignores. As Kent tries to phone the hotel manager the boy pulls the telephone out of the wall and moves downstage to make grimacing faces at the audience. When Kent goes to confront the boy he spits at Kent who runs off to clean himself in the shower. Left alone with the boy Salem then starts to tell him this story.

SALEM. When I was about ten I think, little boy, I'd just returned home from a car trip to the county fair with my family. My father, my mother, my sisters and brothers. We'd just gotten home after driving for about two hours, and it had just gotten dark, but none of us had spoken for the whole trip. Are you listening? It was the same as though we'd all been asleep, and we drove in the driveway, and my father stopped the car. But instead of any of us getting out right away like we usually did we all just sat in the car staring ahead and not speaking for a very long time. I was the first to get out and start walking toward the cement steps that led to the porch and I could hear my family behind me. My father, my mother, my sisters and brothers. And I could hear all four doors of the car slam one after the other like gun shots from a rifle. And I could hear their feet following me up the stairs to the porch right behind me. Very silent. I was leading them sort of and I was only about ten years old. I got

70

to the top of the stairs and I was standing on the porch. I was the first one there and I turned to see them and they all looked right at me. All staggered because of the steps, and all their eyes staring right at me. I saw them like that just for a second, and then do you know what I did little boy? I spit on the very top step just before my father stepped down. And just as he stepped on that little spot of spit that had nothing dirtier in it than cotton candy and caramel apple, my whole family burst into noise like you never ever heard. And my father took off his belt that he'd just bought at the county fair. A black leather belt with a silver buckle and a picture of Trigger engraved on the front. And my father took one more step to the top of the porch with the belt hanging down from his right hand and the buckle clinking on the cement. Then he swung his arm around slowly behind his back so that the belt dragged through the air following his wrist and came back so fast that all I could hear was a crack as it hit my ankles and knees and I fell. Then they were silent again and waited there on the steps until my father put the belt back through the loops and buckled the buckle and hitched his jeans up over his hips. Then they all went into the house in a line. My father first, my mother second, my sisters and brothers third. And I stayed there in a ball, all rolled up, with my knees next to my chin and my hands rubbing my ankles. And I felt very good that they'd left me there by myself.

COMMENTARY: Sam Shepard's great gift is his ability to create daringly combustible plays that are exercises in free-association. He collides social and political themes to achieve a unique dramatic style and vocabulary. His language flickers with life, shifting suddenly from one plane of reality to another. *La Turista* is one of his earliest stage plays, but already his taste for range roving in and around the American psyche is on full display. Shepard shows a satirical cartoonist's glee in the way he boldly portrays his native land and its people. Kent and Salem are typical tourists abroad who stupidly drink the water. They are also a couple of brand named, low-tar American cigarettes.

Salem tells a very complete story about an indelible childhood event, an act of defiance. She tells it simply because she is telling the story to a child. The climax of the speech is the spit followed by the slap across the face. Shot-like sounds are very crucial in this speech and signal menace. With the simplest of means the actor can create the impact of the speech by just following its carefully laid path. Each word and image must be clearly articulated so that the tension mounts. As part of her unemotional narration, notice how she repeats three times her family litany, 'My father, my mother, my sisters and brothers'. It sounds like a police line-up. The performance of this monologue requires a minimum of physicality. It calls for a focused and restrained delivery. The actor should make the audience feel as if they're part of a family watching an old home movie with one memorable incident.

The Lark

(1953) Jean Anouilh

Part 1. A simple, neutral setting. Rouen, France. Early fifteenth century.

Joan of Arc (18) is on trial for heresy and witchcraft. She begins her defence with this, her first speech in the play. She is dressed simply in men's clothes. Her judges, the English Earl of Warwick and Cauchon, the French Bishop of Beauvais, are eager to bring her trial to a quick conclusion.

JOAN. May I begin wherever I like?
[CAUCHON. Yes.]
I like remembering the beginning: at home, in the fields, when I was still a little girl looking after the sheep, the first time I heard the Voices, that is what I like to remember. . . . It is after the evening Angelus. I am very small and my hair is still in pigtails. I am sitting in the field, thinking of nothing at all. God is good and keeps me safe and happy, close to my mother and my father and my brother, in the quiet countryside of Domremy, while the English soldiers are looting and burning villages up and down the land. My big sheep-dog is lying with his head in my lap; and suddenly I feel his body ripple and tremble, and a hand seems to have touched my shoulder, though I know no one has touched me, and the voice says –
[SOMEONE IN THE CROWD. Who is going to be the voice?
JOAN. I am, of course.] I turned to look. A great light was filling the shadows behind me. The voice was gentle and grave. I had never heard it before, and all it said to me was:

73

'Be a good and sensible child, and go often to church.' But I *was* good, and I *did* go to church often, and I showed I was sensible by running away to safety. That was all that happened the first time. And I didn't say anything about it when I got home; but after supper I went back. The moon was rising; it shone on the white sheep; and that was all the light there was. And then came the second time; the bells were ringing for the noonday Angelus. The light came again, in bright sunlight, but brighter than the sun, and that time I saw him.

[CAUCHON. You saw whom?]

A man in a white robe, with two white wings reaching from the sky to the ground. He didn't tell me his name that day, but later on I found that he was the blessed St. Michael.

[WARWICK. Is it absolutely necessary to have her telling these absurdities all over again?

CAUCHON. Absolutely necessary, my lord. (WARWICK *goes back to his corner in silence, and smells the rose he has in his hand.*)]

(*In the deep voice of the Archangel*). – Joan, go to the help of the King of France, and give him back his kingdom. (*She replies in her own voice.*) Oh sir, you haven't looked at me; I am only a young peasant girl, not a great captain who can lead an army. – You will go and search out Robert de Beaudricourt, the Governor of Vaucouleurs. He will give you a suit of clothes to dress you like a man, and he will take you to the Dauphin. St. Catherine and St. Margaret will protect you. (*She suddenly drops to the floor sobbing with fear.*) – Please, please pity me, holy sir! I'm a little girl; I'm happy here alone in the fields. I've never had to be responsible for anything, except my sheep. The Kingdom of France is far beyond anything I can do. If you will only look at me you will see I am small, and ignorant. The realm of France is too heavy, sir. But the King of France has famous Captains, as strong as you could need and they're used to doing these things. If they lose a battle they sleep as soundly as ever.

74

They simply say the snow or the wind was against them; and they just cross all the dead men off their roll. But I should always remember I had killed them. Please have pity on me! . . . No such thing. No pity. He had gone already, and there I was, with France on my shoulders.

Translation by Christopher Fry

COMMENTARY: Anouilh's treatment of Joan of Arc and her story is very sympathetic and upbeat. *The Lark* avoids all the nastiness of Joan's burning at the stake and is far more romantic than Shaw's intellectual treatment of the same material (*see page 118*). Anouilh's optimistic approach to the story is summarized in the final words of the play, '. . . it isn't the painful and miserable end of the cornered animal caught at Rouen: but the lark singing in the open sky. Joan at Reims in all her glory. The true end of the story is a kind of joy.' This feeling of joy permeates the whole play and reflects on Joan's character. Through a series of flashbacks the drama covers Joan's life from childhood to the triumphant coronation of her king, Charles VII, at Reims.

This is the first time Joan speaks in the play. She enjoys recounting the story of her life. Notice how much she relishes the act of performing. She insists on doing all the voices herself. She starts by giving the audience all the good and pleasant bits, all the innocence and especially the light. Nothing is seen in a bad light. The repetition of the light metaphor fills the speech with brightness. Right from the start of the play Joan is saintly and naive, full of confident integrity. The actor has to capture that sanctity for her judges and leave them in no doubt that they are in the presence of a simple peasant girl touched by divinity. Anouilh never tries to explain Joan in psychological terms. Instead he presents her as a phenomenon, a pure spiritual force; the actor should try to find a way to convey this. She uses short, clear sentences to make her points. Imagine the speech practically lifting you off the stage. The images in the speech of white robes and spreading wings help to recreate that moment of transport. Joan must effortlessly bear the entire weight of the French cause on her shoulders.

Long Day's Journey into Night
(1940) Eugene O'Neill

Act 3. Living room of James Tyrone's summer house. August 1912. Half-past six in the evening.

Mary Tyrone (54) 'still has a young, graceful figure, a trifle plump. . . . Her face is distinctly Irish in type. It must once have been extremely pretty. . . . What strikes one immediately is her extreme nervousness. Her hands are never still. They were once beautiful hands, with long tapering fingers, but rheumatism has knotted the joints and warped the fingers, so that now they have an ugly crippled look. One avoids looking at them, the more so because one is conscious she is sensitive about their appearance and humiliated by her inability to control the nervousness which draws attention to them. . . . Her most appealing quality is the simple, unaffected charm of a shy convent-girl youthfulness she has never lost – an innate worldly innocence.' She and her husband James Tyrone have two grown-up sons, Jamie and Edmund. Although a famous and successful actor, Tyrone is miserly. As an economy, when Mary gave birth to Edmund, he summoned an unreliable quack doctor. As a result Mary became a nervous invalid addicted to morphine. Her addiction, which she tries to hide, is aggravated by feelings of guilt about Jamie's alcoholism and Edmund's incurable consumption. In this scene, with Tyrone and Edmund, Mary is full of recrimination and memories about Tyrone's drinking. Tyrone asks her to forget, and she replies with this speech.

MARY (*with detached pity*). [No, dear.] But I forgive. I always forgive you. So don't look so guilty. I'm sorry I remembered out loud. I don't want to be sad, or to make you sad. I want to remember only the happy part of the past. (*Her manner drifts back to the shy, gay convent girl.*) Do you remember our wedding, dear? I'm sure you've completely forgotten what my wedding gown looked like. Men don't

76

notice such things. They don't think they're important. But it was important to me, I can tell you! How I fussed and worried! I was so excited and happy! My father told me to buy anything I wanted and never mind what it cost. The best is none too good, he said. I'm afraid he spoiled me dreadfully. My mother didn't. She was very pious and strict. I think she was a little jealous. She didn't approve of my marrying – especially an actor. I think she hoped I would become a nun. She used to scold my father. She'd grumble, 'You never tell me, never mind what it costs, when I buy anything! You've spoiled that girl so, I pity her husband if she ever marries. She'll expect him to give her the moon. She'll never make a good wife.' (*She laughs affectionately.*) Poor mother! (*She smiles at* TYRONE *with a strange, incongruous coquetry.*) But she was mistaken, wasn't she, James? I haven't been such a bad wife, have I?

[TYRONE (*huskily, trying to force a smile*). I'm not complaining, Mary.]

(*A shadow of vague guilt crosses her face*). At least I've loved you dearly, and done the best I could – under the circumstances. (*The shadow vanishes and her shy, girlish expression returns.*) That wedding gown was nearly the death of me and the dressmaker too! (*She laughs.*) I was so particular. It was never quite good enough. At last she said she refused to touch it any more or she might spoil it, and I made her leave so I could be alone to examine myself in the mirror. I was so pleased and vain. I thought to myself, 'Even if your nose and mouth and ears are a trifle too large, your eyes and hair and figure, and your hands, make up for it. You're just as pretty as any actress he's ever met, and you don't have to use paint.' (*She pauses, wrinkling her brow in an effort of memory.*) Where is my wedding gown now, I wonder? I kept it wrapped up in tissue paper in my trunk. I used to hope I would have a daughter and when it came time for her to marry – she couldn't have bought a lovelier gown, and I knew, James, you'd never tell her, never mind the cost. You'd want her to pick up something at a bargain. It was made of soft, shimmering satin, trimmed with wonderful old duchesse lace, in tiny ruffles around the neck and sleeves, and worked in with the folds that were draped round in a bustle effect at the back. The basque was boned and very tight. I remember I held my breath when it was fitted, so my waist would be as small as possible. My father even let me have duchesse lace on my white satin slippers, and lace with the orange blossoms in my veil. Oh, how I loved that gown! It was so beautiful! Where is it now, I wonder? I used to take it out from time to time when I was lonely, but it always made me cry, so finally a long while ago – (*She wrinkles her forehead again.*) I wonder where I hid it? Probably in one of the old trunks in that attic. Some day I'll have to look. (*She stops, staring before her.*)

COMMENTARY: *Long Day's Journey into Night* is Eugene O'Neill's most autobiographical play. It is generally considered to be his best play in purely dramatic terms. In Mary Tyrone, O'Neill created his most compelling and fully realized female character. O'Neill's aim was to take the audience through the lived experience of a family as they pass nearly twenty-four hours in each other's fitful company. Each member of the family is haunted by their memories of the past. All their loves and hates are combined in equal measures to show an embattled family seeking accord but finding only new evidence for deep discord. Through a series of strategically divulged revelations, the sins of the past play havoc with the present.

This speech focuses on a happy, tender moment and an object. It is also a temporary truce in the war between the Tyrones. The dress offers the actor a beautiful image to play with: its texture, feel and size must take on a reality and give comfort. This detailed memory has a very tangible quality for Mary. The character's relationship to it changes during the course of the speech. Mary is a drug addict and when on morphine (as she is at this moment) she enters a dreamy state of reverie. She talks far longer and more precociously than she should. O'Neill describes the quality of her speech for the actor, 'Her voice is soft and attractive. When she is merry, there is a touch of Irish lilt in it.' Here she seems younger, more girlish and flirtatious. In this play all the characters are artificially stimulated to tell their tales which take them and the audience on a journey to the heart of the matter. What the audience ought to feel from a speech like this is that Mary's wedding day was the happiest single moment in her life. This is a memory that she returns to for comfort over and over again.

Look Back in Anger
(1956) John Osborne

Act 2, scene 1. The Porters' one-room flat in a large Midland town.
Evening. April.

*Alison (24) has been married for three years to Jimmy Porter, a
working-class graduate. She comes from a protected upper-class
background. Her childhood was spent in India where her father was a
Colonel in the army. Jimmy delights in taunting her as his domestic
representative of everything he despises about class, privilege and
women. They share their dreary flat with Cliff, Jimmy's partner with
whom he runs a stall selling sweets in the local market. 'Hers is the most
elusive personality to catch in the uneasy polyphony of these three
people. She is turned in a different key, a key of well-bred malaise that
is often drowned in the robust orchestration of the other two . . . She is
tall, slim, dark. The bones of her face are long and delicate. There is a
surprising reservation about her eyes, which are so large and deep they
should make equivocation impossible.' Alison invites her friend
Helena, an actress, to stay while the latter is appearing in a play at a
local theatre. She confesses to Helena that she is expecting a baby and
that she hasn't told Jimmy yet. In this scene Helena questions her about
Jimmy.*

[HELENA. It's almost unbelievable. I don't understand
your part in it all. Why? That's what I don't see. Why did
you – ?]
ALISON. Marry him? There must be about six different
answers. When the family came back from India, everything
seemed, I don't know – unsettled? Anyway, Daddy seemed
remote and rather irritable. And Mummy – well, you know
Mummy. I didn't have much to worry about. I didn't know I
was born as Jimmy says. I met him at a party. I remember it
so clearly. I was almost twenty-one. The men there all

looked as though they distrusted him, and as for the women, they were all intent on showing their contempt for this rather odd creature, but no one seemed quite sure how to do it. He'd come to the party on a bicycle, he told me, and there was oil all over his dinner jacket. It had been such a lovely day, and he'd been in the sun. Everything about him seemed to burn, his face, the edges of his hair glistened and seemed to spring off his head, and his eyes were so blue and full of the sun. He looked so young and frail, in spite of the tired line of his mouth. I knew I was taking on more than I was ever likely to be capable of bearing, but there never seemed to be any choice. Well, the howl of outrage and astonishment went up from the family, and that did it. Whether or no he was in love with me, that did it. He made up his mind to marry me. They did just about everything they could think of to stop us.

[HELENA. Yes, it wasn't a very pleasant business. But you can see their point.]

Jimmy went into battle with his axe swinging round his head – frail, and so full of fire. I had never seen anything like it. The old story of the knight in shining armour – except that his armour didn't really shine very much.

COMMENTARY: Osborne's *Look Back in Anger* detonated an explosive charge that changed the course of British drama when it was first produced at the Royal Court Theatre in 1956. Jimmy Porter, impotent with rage at all he sees, became the symbol of the disaffected and 'angry young man' of the post-war years. The play broke with the affected, polite traditions of the British stage where orderly drawing room plays ruled the day. Osborne dared to be both profane and uncouth. Playwrights like Harold Pinter, Simon Gray and Peter Nichols have all, in some way, followed the bilious path laid by Osborne.

Jimmy Porter represented an escape for Alison. He was an odd man out, the complete opposite of everything in Alison's life and background. Notice how Jimmy comes across as a force of nature. Alison even gives him god-like characteristics. She, however, seems to be a passive agent in the whole affair. She is swept-up in Jimmy's flow and just follows the current. The actor must decide for herself what Alison's real feelings are towards Jimmy. This speech never reveals those attitudes. There may be a clue in her two references to Jimmy's 'frail' boyish qualities. Throughout the play Alison shows a long-suffering ability to withstand mental cruelty, taunts and insults. She patiently and passively endures what she calls his 'guerilla warfare'. She lacks the education that Jimmy possesses so she lacks the language to fight back.

The Maids
(1947) Jean Genet

One act. Madame's Louis-Quinze style bedroom.

Solange Lemercier (30–35) works alongside her younger sister, Claire, as a housemaid in Madame's house. Throughout the action they indulge in a deadly and perverse game of role-reversing in which they impersonate one another and their hated mistress, and then take turns ritually killing her in mock murders. They seek revenge on Madame by denouncing her lover, Monsieur, to the police, but this plot fails when he is released without charge. The two sisters also feel deep jealousy, hatred and suspicion towards one another. In this speech Solange fantasizes that she has murdered Claire. She creates a vivid fictional scenario for herself and addresses herself to imaginary on-stage characters – Madame and her lover Monsieur and an Inspector.

SOLANGE. Madame. . . . At last! Madame is dead! . . . laid out on the linoleum . . . strangled by the dish-gloves.[1] What? Oh, Madame may remain seated.[2] . . . Madame may call me Mademoiselle Solange. . . . Exactly. It's because of what I've done. Madame and Monsieur will call me Mademoiselle Solange Lemercier. . . . Madame should have taken off that black dress. It's grotesque. (*She imitates* MADAME's *voice.*) So I'm reduced to wearing mourning for my maid. As I left the cemetery all the servants of the neighbourhood marched past me as if I were a member of the family. I've so often been part of the family. Death will see the joke through to the bitter end. . . . What? Oh!

---

[1] **Madame . . . dish-gloves** Solange here is referring to the murdered Claire as 'Madame.' In their role-reversal games Claire portrayed 'Madame'.

[2] **Madame may remain seated** Solange is now imagining herself addressing her real mistress M lame

83

Madame needn't feel sorry for me. I'm Madame's equal and I hold my head high. . . . Oh! And there are things Monsieur doesn't realise. He doesn't know that he used to obey our orders. (*She laughs.*) Ah! Ah! Monsieur was a tiny little boy. Monsieur toed the line when we threatened. No, Inspector, no. . . . I won't talk! I won't say a word. I refuse to speak about our[3] complicity in this murder. . . . The dresses? Oh, Madame could have kept them. My sister and I had our own. Those we used to put on at night, in secret. Now, I have my own dress, and I'm your equal. I wear the red garb of criminials. Monsieur's laughing at me? He's smiling at me. Monsieur thinks I'm mad. He's thinking maids should have better taste than to make gestures reserved for Madame! Monsieur really forgives me? Monsieur is the soul of kindness. He'd like to vie with me in grandeur. But I've scaled the fiercest heights. Madame now sees my loneliness – at last! Yes, I am alone. And fearsome. I might say cruel things, but I can be kind. . . . Madame will get over her fright. She'll get over it well enough. What with her flowers and perfumes and gowns and jewels and lovers. As for me, I've my sister. . . . Yes. I dare speak of these things. I do, Madame. There's nothing I won't dare. And who could silence me, who? Who would be so bold as to say to me: 'My dear child!' I've been a servant. Well and good. I've made the gestures a servant must make. I've smiled at Madame. I've bent down to make the bed, bent down to scrub the tiles, bent down to peel the vegetables, to listen at doors, to glue my eye to keyholes! But now I stand upright. And firm. I'm the strangler. Mademoiselle Solange, the one who strangled her sister! . . . Me be still? Madame is delicate, really. But I pity Madame. I pity Madame's whiteness, her satiny skin, and her little ears, and little

[3] **Our** Solange throughout the play speaks on behalf of herself and Claire, creating a collective self. (Notice this use again later in the speech, 'That's our business' and 'That, my child, is our darkness, ours'.)

84

wrists. . . . Eh? I'm the black crow. . . . Oh! Oh! I have my
judges. I belong to the police. Claire? She was really very
fond of Madame. . . . YOUR dresses again! And THAT
white dress, THAT one, which I forbade her to put on, the
one you wore the night of the Opera Ball, the night you
poked fun at her, because she was sitting in the kitchen
admiring a photo of Gary Cooper. . . . Madame will remember. Madame will remember her gentle irony, the maternal
grace with which she took the magazine from us, and smiled.
Nor will Madame forget that she called her Clarinette.
Monsieur laughed until the tears rolled down his cheeks.
. . . Eh? Who am I? The monstrous soul of servantdom! No,
Inspector, I'll explain nothing in their presence. That's *our*
business. It would be a fine thing if masters could pierce the
shadows where servants live. . . . That, my child, is our
darkness, ours. (*She lights a cigarette and smokes clumsily. The
smoke makes her cough.*) Neither you nor anyone else will be
told anything. Just tell yourselves that this time Solange has
gone through with it. . . . You see her dressed in red. She is
going out. (*She goes to the window, opens it, and steps out on the
balcony. Facing the night, with her back to the audience, she
delivers the following speech. A slight breeze makes the curtains
stir.*) Going out. Descending the great stairway.
Accompanied by the police. Out on your balconies to see her
making her way among the shadowy penitents! It's noon.
She's carrying a nine-pound torch. The hangman follows
close behind. He's whispering sweet nothings in her ear.
Claire! The hangman's by my side! Now take your hand off
my waist. He's trying to kiss me! Let go of me! Ah! Ah! (*She
laughs.*) The hangman's trifling with me. She will be led in
procession by all the maids of the neighbourhood, by all the
servants who accompanied Claire to her final resting place.
They'll all be wearing crowns, flowers, streamers, banners.
They'll toll the bell. The funeral will unfold its pomp. It's
beautiful, isn't it? First come the butlers, in full livery, but
without silk lining. Then come the footmen, the lackeys in

knee breeches and stockings. They're wearing their crowns. Then come the valets, and then the chambermaids wearing our colours. Then the porters. And then come the delegations from heaven. And I'm leading them. The hangman's lulling me. I'm being acclaimed. I'm pale and I'm about to die. . . . (*She returns to the room.*) And what flowers! They gave her such a lovely funeral, didn't they? Oh! Claire, poor little Claire! (*She bursts into tears and collapses into an armchair.*) What? (*She gets up.*) It's no use, Madame, I'm obeying the police. They're the only ones who understand me. They too belong to the world of outcasts, the world you touch only with tongs. (*Visible only to the audience,* CLAIRE, *during the last few moments, has been leaning with her elbows against the jamb of the kitchen door and listening to her sister.*) Now we are Mademoiselle Solange Lemercier, that Lemercier woman. The famous criminal. And above all, Monsieur need not be uneasy. I'm not a maid. I have a noble soul. . . . (*She shrugs her shoulders.*) No, no, not another word, my dear fellow. Ah, Madame's not forgetting what I've done for her. . . . No, no she must not forget my devotion. . . . (*Meanwhile* CLAIRE *enters through the door at the left. She is wearing the white dress.*) And in spite of my forbidding it, Madame continues to stroll about the apartment. She will please sit down . . . and listen to me. . . . (*To* CLAIRE.) Claire . . . we're raving!

Translation by Bernard Frechtman

COMMENTARY: The world of a Genet play is conceived as a macabre cabaret in which fantasy and wish fulfilment play crucial roles. In *The Maids* (the ultimate in master/servant relationship plays) black humour, transformational characterization, quick costume changes and a rich interplay of light, colour and emotions together create a tantalizing hall of mirrors for the audience. Our tame, civilised notions about human behaviour, identity and morality are thrown into doubt. In this grotesque carnival, Genet reveals woman's immorality to woman. The audience is asked to see a fractured view of themselves with all their secret desires and darkest humiliations exposed in the process.

The actor is the chief vehicle in this enterprise. This is Solange's great chance to voice all the resentments, frustrations and jealousies of her subjection and submission. She is indulging in a potent fantasy as she asserts her independent identity. Solange plays many roles, many versions of herself: a sister, a maid, a lover, her Madame and a murderess. She concocts a bizarre and sometimes schizophrenic pageant of subplots and counterplots. The murder and funeral she describes are just further charades. The actor must convince the audience that what they are hearing and seeing while she is in these different guises is real. The image of the dress is used as a talisman, conjuring up alternative notions of religious purity and sullied degradation. There can be no denying that the speech is also like a surreal nightmare. The progress of the narrative journey has a rather gothic fury that should engage the performer at every turn. At all costs try to avoid a psychological or naturalistic interpretation of the speech. That will only freeze you in your tracks and reduce Genet's speculative theatrical exuberance to a single level of meaning.

The Misunderstanding
(1944) Albert Camus

Act 3. The clean, brightly lit public room of an inn in Bohemia.

Martha (20s) lives with her mother who runs an inn in a dreary, isolated town. Martha dreams of escaping to the sea with a rich man. The two women have a habit of murdering and then robbing their male guests. They drug their victims and drown them in the river. They feel no guilt: their only scruple is that it is too tiring. They aim to accumulate enough money so that they can run away and start new lives. Jan, Martha's older brother, returns unexpectedly after an absence of twenty years, to bring them money and 'some happiness'. However, when neither of the women recognise him, he decides to behave like an ordinary traveller. They resolve that this guest will be their last victim. The morning after the murder, upon finding Jan's passport, they finally realize the tragic identity of their victim. The Mother responds with sincere grief and leaves to kill herself. Martha cannot understand this emotion, and left alone bitterly reflects on her situation.

MARTHA (*once her* MOTHER *has left she runs to the door, slams it to, and presses herself against it. She breaks into loud, fierce cries*). No, no! What concern of mine was it to look after my brother? None whatever! And yet now I'm an outcast in my own home, there is no place for me to lay my head, my own mother will have none of me. No, it wasn't my duty to look after him – oh, the unfairness of it all, the injustice done to innocence! For he – he now has what he wanted, while I am left lonely, far from the sea I longed for. Oh, how I hate him! All my life was spent waiting for this great wave that was to lift me up and sweep me far away, and now I know it will never come again. I am doomed to stay here with all those other countries, other nations, on my left hand and my

88

right, before me and behind; all those plains and mountains that are barriers to the salt winds blowing from the sea, and whose chatterings and grumblings drown its low, unceasing summons. (*In a lower tone.*) There are places to which, far as they may be from the sea, the evening wind brings sometimes a smell of seaweed. It tells of moist seabeaches, loud with the cries of seagulls, or of golden sands bathed in a sunset glow that has no limit. But the sea winds fail long before they reach this place. Never, never shall I have what's due to me. I may press my ear to the earth but I shall not hear the crash of icy breakers, or the measured breathing of a happy sea. I am too far from all I love, and my exile is beyond remedy. I hate him, yes, I hate him for having got what he wanted! My only home is in this gloomy, shut-in country where the sky has no horizons; for my hunger I have nothing but the sour Moravian sloes,* for my thirst only the blood that I have shed. That is the price one must pay for a mother's love! There is no love for me, so let her die. Let every door be shut against me; all I wish is to be left in peace with my anger, my very rightful anger. For I have no intention of rolling my eyes heavenward or pleading for forgiveness before I die. In that southern land, guarded by the sea, to which one can escape, where one can breathe freely, press one's body to another's body, roll in the waves — to that sea-guarded land the gods have no access. But here one's gaze is cramped on every side, everything is planned to make one look up in humble supplication. I hate this narrow world in which we are reduced to gazing up at God. But I have not been given my rights and I am smarting from the injustice done me; I will not bend my knee. I have been cheated of my place on earth, cast away by my mother, left alone with my crimes, and I shall leave this world without being reconciled.

Translation by Stuart Gilbert

*sloes bluish black berries that produce a bitter juice

COMMENTARY: In *The Misunderstanding* Camus wanted to fashion an austere modern tragedy on the classical theme of destiny. Camus chose a very mundane setting and ordinary characters to tell his nightmarish story. In order to achieve his aim he created a stark, claustrophobic world in which fate battles with human free will. It is the engagement between these two forces – plus a simple case of mistaken identity – that obsesses the characters in the end. Tension evolves as misunderstanding is heaped on misunderstanding with great ironic significance.

In this speech Martha reveals all her dreams, fears and aspirations. She recognizes the inevitable doom that will follow from her act. Notice how she begins her speech on high and gradually takes her voice lower and lower in a physical process that matches her tragic downfall. In stark words Martha reveals herself as a solitary figure. She paints a picture of the desolate, featureless landscape that imprisons her. By contrast notice how passionate and lyrical she becomes when she vividly describes the sun-filled seascape of her dreams. In stature and power this speech matches the best lamentations of classical tragedy though the key is that of modern existentialism. Martha has shaped her destiny through her own choice and action even though the outcome is absurd. She is guided by neither religious nor moral scruples. The actor must convey Martha's fervent conviction in all that she says, although her reasoning is deeply and disquietingly irrational. She feels cheated by fate but continues to assert her free will and shape her own destiny in an apparently random world. She faces a very lonely end, friendless and bereft of family. Martha seeks happiness but is thwarted by fate and her own presumption.

Napoli Milionaria
(1945) Eduardo de Filippo

Act 2. A large cyclamen coloured room in a Neapolitan house, 1944.

Assunta (24), a working-class Italian woman, lives in a bustling, crowded quarter of Naples. She is 'naive, open and a little bit scatty. Assunta is apt to go into hysterical laughter for no apparent reason in the middle of a sentence. She is in mourning for a soldier-husband she believes is dead and wears a simple black dress with black ear-rings.' She calls on her neighbour, Amalia, for some 'worldly advice'.

[AMALIA. Assunta, I have to tell you there are times when you drive me clean up the wall.]
ASSUNTA. I know. I can't help it. I do it to everyone. I think I must have a weakness somewhere. (*Struggles desperately to control her laughter. Finally succeeds.*) There. It's over now. Fingers crossed, eh? Right. Well, what I wanted to ask you was . . . well, I was going to ask Aunt Adelaide, but she knows less than I do about it, and what with you being a woman of the world and . . .
[AMALIA. For heaven's sake, spit it out, will you.]
Yes. Right. Well, what I wanted to know is this – am I a virgin?
[AMALIA. How in God's name am I supposed to know?]
Well, the thing is, you see, the thing is I got married by proxy.
[AMALIA. What?]
To Ernesto Santafede on the twenty-fourth of March 1941. He was on military service, you see, and . . . isn't that a lovely dress? Is it new?

[AMALIA. Yes. The dressmaker came round with it special yesterday. Now get on with it, will you?]

Yes, certainly. Well, the thing is, you see, he had to go off to North Africa while we were engaged, and that was the last thing I saw of him till after we were married. But we never got together properly as husband and wife, you see, because when he came back home on fourteen days leave, we were supposed to have this room all to ourselves. Oh, it was a lovely room. Aunt Adelaide had done it up special with clean sheets so we could . . . we could . . . well, you know – so we could be alone. It was so romantic. I'd got myself all dolled up really nice. I used up a whole bottle of scent and then . . . (*Mimics sound of air raid sirens.*) . . . well, we had no time to do anything except make a bolt for the shelter. We were down there the whole fortnight he was on leave. And then he had to go back. And I haven't seen or heard of him since. Actually I tell a lie. He did get a message through once. He didn't send it personal. It came via this cousin by marriage of a friend of mine who was in Rome at the time. And he bumped into this old lady who happened to be coming through Naples on her way to Calabria and . . .

[AMALIA. Yes, yes, yes. But what was the message?]

Well, there was nothing to it really. She said he'd been taken prisoner. And then a friend of his who'd come back from the front said he'd been killed. And then someone else said they'd seen him alive. And then someone else said . . . So what I'm asking is this – am I technically a virgin or not? . . . I don't want to get married again. I couldn't anyway. Out of respect. (*Shows* AMALIA *her husband's photograph in a locket she's wearing round her neck.*) See? That's him. The one with the bemused expression. That's why I always wear mourning. Except when someone comes along and tells me he's alive. Then I take it off. Then someone else says, no, he isn't, and back it goes on again. It's on off, on off all the time. It's making me dizzy. It's ridiculous. I just want to be one thing or the other. Not that anyone notices. Who cares about me? Who gives a fig?

Translation by Peter Tinniswood

COMMENTARY: Eduardo de Filippo's Neapolitan comedies are naturalistic domestic dramas rich in humour and colloquial dialogue. As an actor-playwright with his own company de Filippo was well aware of the needs of the actor. He created roles and dialogue which invite the actor to shine in performance. All of his characters exist on an emotional plane, displaying their anxieties, frustrations and silliness while trying to maintain an existence in hard times. *Napoli Milionaria* follows the exploits of common people who set up a black market enterprise in the midst of the Second World War.

Assunta is a comic bundle of nerves and hysteria. She drives people crazy and is easily distracted from her main point. Her immaturity is evident at every turn; what she knows about the facts of life is distressingly vague. She has never slept with a man and perhaps has never ventured far beyond the quarter in which she lives. You can see that she's led a sheltered existence and seems more like a girl than a mature woman. Her tale has a breathless quality where idea follows idea without much logic or order: 'and then . . . and then . . . and then . . .' She accelerates, decelerates and accelerates again, thinking and talking by stops and starts. She desperately wants answers, but in her embarrassed gabbing she leaves no chance for anyone to get a word in edgeways. The actor might think of ways to physicalise Assunta's awkwardness and how Assunta might try to keep Amalia's attention and good will. In a way Assunta has not only married by proxy but has lived her life that way also.

Old Times
(1971) Harold Pinter

Act 1. The sitting-room of a converted farmhouse. Autumn. Night.

Anna (30s–40s) is Kate's former best friend and flat mate. She has come to visit Kate and her husband Deeley. The two women have not seen one another for several years. Kate and Deeley have been discussing Anna and how they came to know her; Deeley, however, maintains that he has never met Anna. This speech is the first time Anna speaks in the play.

ANNA (*turns from the window, speaking, and moves down to them, eventually sitting on the second sofa*). Queuing all night, the rain, do you remember? my goodness, the Albert Hall, Covent Garden, what did we eat? to look back, half the night, to do things we loved, we were young then of course, but what stamina, and to work in the morning, and to a concert, or the opera, or the ballet, that night, you haven't forgotten? and then riding on top of the bus down Kensington High Street, and the bus conductors, and then dashing for the matches for the gasfire and then I suppose scrambled eggs, or did we? who cooked? both giggling and chattering, both huddling to the heat, then bed and sleeping, and all the hustle and bustle in the morning, rushing for the bus again for work, lunchtimes in Green Park, exchanging all our news, with our very own sandwiches, innocent girls, innocent secretaries, and then the night to come, and goodness knows what excitement in store, I mean the sheer expectation of it all, the looking-forwardness of it all, and so poor, but to be poor and young, and a girl, in London then

. . . and the cafés we found, almost private ones, weren't they? where artists and writers and sometimes actors collected, and others with dancers, we sat hardly breathing with our coffee, heads bent, so as not to be seen, so as not to disturb, so as not to distract, and listened and listened to all those words, all those cafés and all those people, creative undoubtedly, and does it still exist I wonder? do you know? can you tell me?

COMMENTARY: Pinter's *Old Times* is a curious triangular play about romances and encounters that may or may not have happened. The audience is always left in doubt by the oblique manner in which the characters speak. Whatever they say is open to innumerable interpretations, giving the play a mysterious, playful quality.

Anna is an enigma. She is the sort of character for whom an actor must supply the biographical details which the playwright omits. Yet Anna has a spellbinding way of speaking. Notice how her speech is really one long sentence composed of private images and clichés. The incidents in her narrative have a fragmentary, dreamlike quality. There seems to be a narrative of sorts but it is punctuated with questions that suddenly throw suspicion on everything that's been said before. How to use this speech is up to the performer. You must back-up each statement with a motive. Anna has almost a ghostly presence. She seems both menacing and innocent. What she says should magnetize the audience who will want to hear her every word, especially since she has been a silent, sphinx-like character for so long. She speeds up phrases, punctuates the action and then slows down for the questions. The speech reads like a riddle in shorthand. She uses no gender pronouns, 'he' or 'she', to indicate who she's shared all these intimate moments with, but whoever it is has a central role in her narrative. Anna is a genuine mystery woman.

Otherwise Engaged
(1975) Simon Gray

Act 2. The living-room of Hench's house in London.

Beth Hench (30s) teaches English to foreign students. She is married to Simon, a successful publisher. They live in a comfortably appointed house in London and have no children to interfere with their sophisticated and urbane lifestyle. Simon maintains a cool, selfish distance, remaining 'otherwise engaged' from all the emotional entanglements of his friends, family and colleagues. He has been unfaithful to Beth on several occasions. While Beth is away on a trip with her students, one of their friends reveals to Simon that Beth is having an affair with her colleague, Ned. Simon, however, has known about this affair for ten months. Beth returns just after this revelation and Simon distances her with verbal barriers. She not only admits to the affair but also that she wants to leave Simon and marry Ned. This is her final outburst.

BETH (*quietly*). You know the most insulting thing, that you let me go on and on being unfaithful without altering your manner or your behaviour one – one – you don't care about me, or my being in love with somebody else, or my betraying you, good God! least of all that! But you do wish I hadn't actually *mentioned* it, because then we could have gone on, at least *you* could, pretending that everything was all right, no, not even pretending, as far as *you* were concerned, everything was all right, you probably still think it *is* all right – and – and – you've – you've – all those times we've made love, sometimes the very same evening as Ned and I – and yet you took me – in your usual considerate fashion, just as you take your third of a bottle of wine with dinner or your carefully measured brandy and your cigar after it, *and* enjoyed it all the more because I felt guilty, God help me *guilty* and so tried harder for your sake – and you *admit* that, no, not admit it, simply state it as if on the difference made by an extra voice or something in your bloody Wagner – don't you see, don't you see that that makes you a freak! You're – you're – oh, damn! Damn. Damn you. (*Pause.*) Oh damn. (*There is a silence.*) So you might as well listen to your Wagner.

COMMENTARY: Simon Gray's *Otherwise Engaged* is a melancholic comedy. There is a keen wit in all of Gray's dramas that harks back to the great Restoration plays of the eighteenth century. Yet the wit and parrying humour are used to disguise deep hurts. His characters love to talk, often using language as an intellectual defence against emotion. They all indulge in destructive games of power and passion, accusation and recrimination.

This speech is placed towards the close of the play. It begins quietly and builds in power before diminishing again at the end. Beth's anger flashes rather than burns at one constant temperature. Remember that the 'otherwise engaged' Simon is her target and she keeps him in focus at all times, firing one accusatory 'you' after another at him. The speech is practically one long breathless sentence. The deepest frustrations and resentments are uncovered in this monologue. At various points along the way Beth, who seems to be getting very little reaction from Simon, loses her way and cannot complete thoughts. Anger for her is an uncharacteristic feeling. It is almost as if saying harsh words is too devastating for her. The actor has to sympathise with her plight and exasperation in order not to make this speech sound hackneyed. Notice how much of her anger is revealed in sharply articulated words like 'actually' and 'bloody'. The normally cool Beth shows stress at a moment of crisis like this.

The Plough and the Stars

(1926) Sean O'Casey

Act 3. The street outside the Clitheroes' house in Dublin. Easter Week, 1916.

Nora Clitheroe is a 'young woman of twenty-two, alert, swift, full of nervous energy, and a little anxious to get on in the world. The firm lines of her face are considerably opposed by a soft amorous mouth and gentle eyes. When her firmness fails her, she persuades with her feminine charm.' She is married to Jack Clitheroe, a bricklayer who is, much against Nora's wishes, a Commandant in the Irish Citizen Army. The other residents of the tenement are also loyal to the Plough and the Stars, the banner of Irish independence. During the violent uprisings of Easter Week, Jack is called up. Nora's distress increases until she starts wandering the streets in search of her husband. In this scene, Fluther, one of her neighbours, risks his life to save her and brings her home, 'Fluther has his arm around her and is half leading, half carrying her in. Her eyes are dim and hollow, her face pale and stained-looking; her hair is tossed and her clothes are dusty.' As her neighbours try to comfort her she reveals her anxieties.

NORA. Oh, I know that wherever he is he's thinkin' of wantin' to be with me. I know he's longin' to be with me. I know he's longin' to be passin' his hand through me hair to be caressin' me neck, to fondle me hand an' to feel me kisses clingin' to his mouth. . . . An' he stands wherever he is because he's brave? (*Vehemently.*) No, but because he's a coward, a coward, a coward!

[MRS GOGAN. Oh, they're not cowards anyway.]

(*With denunciatory anger.*) I tell you they're afraid to say they're afraid! . . . Oh, I saw it, I saw it, Mrs Gogan. . . . At th' barricade in North King Street I saw fear glowin' in all their eyes. . . . An' in the middle o' th' street was somethin'

98

huddled up in a horrible tangled heap. . . . His face was jammed again th' stones, an' his arm was twisted round his back. . . . An' every twist of his body was a cry against th' terrible thing that had happened to him. . . . An' I saw they were afraid to look at it. . . . An' some o' them laughed at me, but th' laugh was a frightened one. . . . An' some o' them shouted at me, but th' shout had in it th' shiver o' fear. . . . I tell you they were afraid, afraid, afraid!

[MRS GOGAN (*leading her towards the house*). Come on in, dear. If you'd been a little longer together, th' wrench assundher wouldn't have been so sharp.]

Th' agony I'm in since he left me has thrust away every rough thing he done, an' every unkind word he spoke; only th' blossoms that grew out of our lives are before me now; shakin' their colours before me face, an' breathin' their sweet scent on every thought springin' up in me mind, till, sometimes, Mrs Gogan, sometimes I think I'm goin' mad! [MRS GOGAN. You'll be a lot betther when you have a little lie down.]

(*Turning towards* FLUTHER *as she is going in*). I don't know what I'd have done, only for Fluther. I'd have been lyin' in th' streets, only for him. . . . (*As she goes in.*) They have dhriven away th' little happiness life had to spare for me. He has gone from me for ever, for ever. . . . Oh, Jack, Jack, Jack!

COMMENTARY: Sean O'Casey's *The Plough and the Stars* exposes the cruelty and waste of war. Nationalist sympathies and the horror of bloodshed allow his characters, even the most lowly, to speak with the lyrical fervour of eye-witnesses. O'Casey is renowned for creating dialogue charged with poetry, rich in idiom and Irish cadences. He reveals how the turmoil of the Easter Rebellion affects his characters by treating each one with equal sympathy and compassion.

Nora is shell-shocked and shaken by the violence she has just barely survived. She puts herself into the mind and place of Jack, trying to experience what he's experiencing. The displacement gives her speech a vivid, moving quality. The images she uses are all grotesque; twisted, tangled figures locked in fear and battle like Goya's nightmarish painted visions of conflict. She has had to confront the horror of war and comes back like a reporter from the front line to tell of what she has seen. Nora is a simple character and not normally poetic. But the need to speak gives her words an unmistakeable lyricism. Notice how starkly her sweet memories of Jack contrast with the harsh images of carnage and waste. The memory is almost an epiphany for her, a breathless paean to love. The final repetition of 'Jack, Jack, Jack' should shake the audience like a volley of rifle shots.

Pygmalion
(1912) Bernard Shaw

Act 5. Mrs Higgins's drawing-room.

Eliza Doolittle (18) starts the play as a wilful Cockney flower-girl. Henry Higgins, the famous professor of phonetics and a confirmed bachelor, observes her selling flowers in Covent Garden. He wagers with Colonel Pickering (another phonetician) that he can transform Eliza into a 'lady' and pass her off as a duchess at a society ball. Eliza decides to accept his offer to transform her, realizing that if she can speak like a lady then she can open her own flower shop. She moves into a room in Higgins' house and he ruthlessly coaches her in the arts of speech and etiquette. Higgins successfully transforms her and wins his wager. Higgins never once thinks of the impact his experiment will have on Eliza herself; he treats her merely as an object. After her debut as a lady at the ball Higgins offers her no praise, instead he asks her to fetch his slippers. It is then that she realizes that she means nothing to Higgins and walks out on him, seeking refuge at his mother's house. Higgins comes in pursuit of her and admits he has 'grown accustomed' to her face. In this speech, addressed to Pickering but equally for Higgins' benefit, she explains, while embroidering, why she prefers Pickering to Higgins.

LIZA. Oh, I'm only a squashed cabbage leaf –
[PICKERING (*impulsively*). No.]
– but I owe so much to you that I should be very unhappy if you forgot me.
[PICKERING. It's very kind of you to say so, Miss Doolittle.]
It's not because you paid for my dresses. I know you are generous to everybody with money. But it was from you that I learnt really nice manners; and that is what makes one a lady, isnt it? You see it was so very difficult for me with the

example of Professor Higgins always before me. I was brought up to be just like him, unable to control myself, and using bad language on the slightest provocation. And I should never have known that ladies and gentlemen didnt behave like that if you hadnt been there.

[HIGGINS. Well!!

PICKERING. Oh, that's only his way, you know. He doesnt mean it.]

Oh, I didnt mean it either, when I was a flower girl. It was only my way. But you see I did it; and thats what makes the difference after all.

[PICKERING. No doubt. Still, he taught you to speak; and I couldnt have done that, you know.

LIZA (*trivially*). Of course: that is his profession.

HIGGINS. Damnation!]

(*Continuing.*) It was like learning to dance in the fashionable way: there was nothing more than that in it. But do you know what began my real education?

[PICKERING. What?]

(*Stopping her work for a moment.*) Your calling me Miss Doolittle that day when I first came to Wimpole Street. That was the beginning of self-respect for me. (*She resumes her stitching.*) And there were a hundred little things you never noticed, because they came naturally to you. Things about standing up and taking off your hat and opening doors –

[PICKERING. Oh, that was nothing.]

Yes: things that shewed you thought and felt about me as if I were something better than a scullery-maid; though of course I know you would have been just the same to a scullery-maid if she had been let into the drawing-room. You never took off your boots in the dining-room when I was there.

[PICKERING. You mustnt mind that. Higgins takes off his boots all over the place.

LIZA. I know.] I am not blaming him. It is his way, isnt it? But it made such a difference to me that you didnt do it. You

102

see, really and truly, apart from the things anyone can pick up (the dressing and the proper way of speaking, and so on) the difference between a lady and a flower girl is not how she behaves, but how she's treated. I shall always be a flower girl to Professor Higgins, because he always treats me as a flower girl, and always will; but I know I can be a lady to you, because you always treat me as a lady and always will. [MRS HIGGINS. Please dont grind your teeth, Henry. PICKERING. Well, this is really very nice of you, Miss Doolittle.] I should like you to call me Eliza, now, if you would. [PICKERING. Thank you, Eliza, of course.] And I should like Professor Higgins to call me Miss Doolittle.

COMMENTARY: Shaw's *Pygmalion* updates the classical myth of Pygmalion and Galatea – the story of an artist who brings a statue to life. The play itself comes to life most passionately and theatrically when it debates and tests ideas about human communication. Higgins transforms Eliza from a vital individual into a petrified model, reversing the process of his mythical counterpart. When Eliza frees herself from Higgins's tutelage her transformation is finally complete. Then she becomes a 'new' woman with her own freedom and independence. In Eliza, Shaw created a marvellous role for an actress.

Eliza's opening sentence and image is a direct quote from Higgins's initial description of her in Covent Garden as a 'squashed cabbage leaf'. Although Eliza is speaking to Pickering (and this speech is more dialogue than monologue) her words are directed always at Henry Higgins. Pickering is only the sounding board. Higgins, however, only really appreciates the sound of his own voice. With Pickering, Eliza can at least shape her thoughts and put them into words. She is a human being seeking respect. For a play about speech and voice, there is actually very little real human communication in the drama. This is precisely the point Eliza raises. Making contact is one of her aims. Without such contact what good are manners and speech? With Pickering she can be friends but with Higgins she demands professional distance and courtesy. Rather than close the communication gap she has widened it.

The Room
(1960) Harold Pinter

One act. A room in a large house.

Clarissa Sands (20s) is married to Toddy Sands and they come to look at a room to let in a dilapidated boarding house. While searching for the landlord they are discovered on the landing by two elderly tenants, Rose and Bert Hudd, who invite them in to warm up. They all chat for a while until Mrs Hudd asks Clarissa if she found anyone in the basement.

MRS SANDS. Yes, Mrs Hudd, you see, the thing is, Mrs Hudd, we'd heard they'd got a room to let here, so we thought we'd come along and have a look. Because we're looking for a place, you see, somewhere quiet, and we knew this district was quiet, and we passed the house a few months ago and we thought it looked very nice, but we thought we'd call of an evening, to catch the landlord, so we came along this evening. Well, when we got here we walked in the front door and it was very dark in the hall and there wasn't anyone about. So we went down to the basement. Well, we got down there only due to Toddy having such good eyesight really. Between you and me, I didn't like the look of it much, I mean the feel, we couldn't make much out, it smelt damp to me. Anyway, we went through a kind of partition, then there was another partition, and we couldn't see where we were going, well, it seemed to me it got darker the more we went, the further we went in, I thought we must have come to the wrong house. So I stopped. And Toddy stopped. And then this voice said, this voice came – it said – well, it gave me a bit of a fright, I don't know about Tod, but someone asked if he could do anything for us. So Tod said we were looking for the landlord and this man said the landlord would be upstairs. Then Tod asked was there a room vacant. And this man, this voice really, I think he was behind the partition, said yes there was a room vacant. He was very polite, I thought, but we never saw him, I don't know why they never put a light on. Anyway, we got out then and we came up and we went to the top of the house. I don't know whether it was the top. There was a door locked on the stairs, so there might have been another floor, but we didn't see anyone, and it was dark, and we were just coming down again when you opened your door.

COMMENTARY: Harold Pinter's *The Room* presents an everyday situation which gradually becomes increasingly mysterious and menacing. *The Room*, in common with Pinter's other early plays, has characters who find themselves in an ambiguous and alien environment. Nothing is certain or quite as it seems. In almost neutral tones his characters describe a world that sounds like something straight out of the pages of Kafka's fiction. Pinter's dialogue combines an authentic, seemingly natural quality with a heightened sense of diction and control.

Mrs Sands explains her story with idiosyncratic precision. Each sentence contains a series of linked explanations. She meticulously mentions every relevant detail. But in all her talking notice how little she actually reveals about herself. Her sentences are a verbal blur. What they relate is a puzzle, a nightmarish sequence of events in which nothing quite makes sense. From her measured, deadpan tone, however, she could just be describing a trip to the supermarket. The central image of the play is a labyrinth full of many halls and doors. Where they lead is anybody's guess. Up seems like down and vice versa. Notice how Mrs Sands punctuates her story with details of every stop and go movement they made on their mystifying search of the house.

Roots
(1959) Arnold Wesker

Act 3. A neat, simple cottage in Norfolk

Beatie Bryant (22) is 'an ample, blonde, healthy-faced young woman'. She comes from Norfolk and her family are poor, uneducated farm labourers. She moves to London to work as a waitress and falls in love with Ronnie Kahn, a Jewish socialist intellectual. He tries to expand her horizons, but she resists his encouragement, revelling in her lack of sophistication and 'learning'. She returns to her parents' cottage for the weekend, with plans that Ronnie will join her. Beatie launches into a criticism of her family, quoting Ronnie at them. She believes that Ronnie plans to marry her. However, he sends a letter breaking off their relationship. Beatie quickly realizes that she failed to live up to his expectations. Her parents refuse to comfort her, taunting her instead. She lashes out at them, blaming them for having no 'roots' and no pride, for living purely from moment to moment. In this speech she suddenly starts to find her own voice.

BEATIE. What do you mean, what am I on about? I'm talking! Listen to me! I'm tellin' you that the world's bin growing for two thousand years and we hevn't noticed it. I'm tellin' you that we don't know what we are or where we come from. I'm telling you something's cut us off from the beginning. I'm telling you we've got no roots. Blimey Joe! We've all got large allotments, we all grow things around us so we should know about roots. You know how to keep your flowers alive don't you Mother? Jimmy - you know how to keep the roots of your veges strong and healthy. It's not only the corn that need strong roots, you know, it's us too. But what've we got? Go on, tell me, what've we got? We don't know where we push up from and we don't bother neither.

[PEARL. Well, I aren't grumbling.

BEATIE. You say you aren't – oh yes, you say so, but look at you.] What've you done since you come in? Hev you said anythin'? I mean really said or done anything to show you're alive? Alive! Blust, what do it mean? Do you know what it mean? Any of you? Shall I tell you what Susie said when I went and saw her? She say she don't care if that ole atom bomb drop and she die – that's what she say. And you know why she say it? I'll tell you why, because if she had to care she'd have to do something about it and she find *that* too much effort. Yes she do. She can't be bothered – she's too bored with it all. That's what we all are – we're all too bored.

[MRS BRYANT. Blust woman – bored you say, bored? You say Susie's bored, with a radio and television an' that? I go t'hell if she's bored!]

Oh yes, we turn on a radio or a TV set maybe, or we go to the pictures – if them's love stories or gangsters – but isn't that the easiest way out? Anything so long as we don't have to make an effort. Well, am I right? You know I'm right. Education ent only books and music – it's asking questions, all the time. There are millions of us, all over the country, and no one, not one of us, is asking questions, we're all taking the easiest way out. Everyone I ever worked with took the easiest way out. We don't fight for anything, we're so mentally lazy we might as well be dead. Blust, we are dead! And you know what Ronnie say sometimes? He say it serves us right! That's what he say – it's our own bloody fault!

[JIMMY. So that's us summed up then – so we know where *we* are then!

MRS BRYANT. Well if he don't reckon we count nor nothin', then it's as well he didn't come. There! It's as well he didn't come.]

Oh, *he* thinks we count all right – living in mystic communion with nature. Living in mystic bloody communion with nature (indeed). But us count? Count Mother? I wonder. Do we? Do you think we really count? You don' wanna take any notice of what them ole papers say about the workers bein' all-important these days – that's all squit! 'Cos we aren't. Do you think when the really talented people in the country get to work they get to work for us? Hell if they do! Do you think they don't know we 'ont make the effort? The writers don't write thinkin' we can understand, nor the painters don't paint expecting us to be interested – that they don't, nor don't the composers give out music thinking we can appreciate it. 'Blust,' they say, 'the masses is too stupid for us to come down to them. Blust,' they say, 'if they don't make no effort why should we bother?' So you know who come along? The slop singers and the pop writers and the film makers and women's magazines and the Sunday papers and the picture strip love stories – that's who come along, and you don't have to make no effort for them, it come easy. 'We know where the money lie,' they say, 'hell we do! The workers've got it so let's give them what they want. If they want slop songs and film idols we'll give 'em that then. If they want words of one syllable, we'll give 'em that then. If they want the third rate, *blust!* We'll give 'em *that* then. Anything's good enough for them 'cos they don't ask for no more!' The whole stinkin' commercial world insults us and we don't care a damn. Well, Ronnie's right – it's our own bloody fault. We want the third-rate – we got it! We got it! We got it! We . . . (*Suddenly* BEATIE *stops as if listening to herself. She pauses, turns with an ecstatic smile on her face –*) D'you hear that? D'you hear it? Did you listen to me? I'm talking. Jenny, Frankie, Mother – I'm not quoting no more. [MRS BRYANT (*getting up to sit at table*). Oh hell, I had enough of her – let her talk a while she'll soon get fed up. (*The others join her at the table and proceed to eat and murmur.*)] Listen to me someone. (*As though a vision were revealed to her.*) God in heaven, *Ronnie!* It does work, it's happening to me, I can feel it's happened, I'm beginning, on my own two feet – I'm beginning.

(*The murmur of the family sitting down to eat grows as*

BEATIE's *last cry is heard. Whatever she will do they will continue to live as before. As* BEATIE *stands alone, articulate at last – the curtain falls.*)

COMMENTARY: Arnold Wesker's *Roots* is the central drama in his landmark trilogy of plays (which begins with *Chicken Soup with Barley* and ends with *I'm Talking About Jerusalem*). Together they form an extraordinary drama of political action and social realism. They follow the declining fortunes of the English socialist movement as its ideals and integrity become increasingly compromised by individuals. Wesker embodies his themes in a highly charged cast of characters.

Beatie speaks with a new found urgency just as the drama reaches its final curtain. She exchanges one set of rural roots for another set based on urban ideas of class conflict and social justice. Beatie is as surprised as everyone else on stage by her sudden explosion. Once she finds her voice, she gets stronger and stronger. She uses each 'blust' to lift her into a higher orbit (she is like one of the new space rockets of the period). Sustaining this speech is a huge challenge. It is crucial that the actor knows exactly where Beatie has come from in the play and why she unleashes such verbal fury. You also have to know who she is talking to and the kind of scores this speech is settling. The speech is consciously meant to have a 'born again' quality; notice that her final word is 'beginning'. Beatie will make a new start because she's suddenly become her own woman. In language she has created her own independence. The monologue draws on the Norfolk dialect and its colloquial power must resonate in any performance.

The Ruffian on the Stair
(1964) Joe Orton

Scene 3. A kitchen/living room with a bedroom alcove. Morning.

Joyce (20s) now a housewife, was once a distinguished prostitute. She tells her husband, Mike, who works as a hired killer, that she has been visited by Wilson, a threatening and mysterious stranger. Mike dismisses her anxieties and fears that Wilson will molest her. He suggests that if she needs help then she should call on Mary, their neighbour from downstairs. Here Joyce dwells on her lonely plight.

JOYCE (*pauses in cleaning the room*). I can't go to the park. I can't sit on cold stone. I might get piles from the lowered temperature. I wouldn't want them on top of everything else. (*She puts down the duster, apathetically.*) I'd try, maybe, a prayer. But the Virgin would turn a deaf ear to a Protestant. (*Pause.*) I can't be as alone as all that. Nobody ought to be. It's heartbreaking. (*She listens. There is silence.*) The number of humiliating admissions I've made. You'd think it would draw me closer to somebody. But it doesn't. (*Three short rings are given on the doorbell.*) Who's there? (*No answer.*) What do you want? (*Making up her mind.*) I'll answer the door to no one. They can hammer it down. (*Pause.*) Is it the milk? (*Calling.*) Are you deaf? No, it wouldn't be him. He only rings for his money. (*She stands behind the door. Loudly.*) Are you the insurance? (*Pause.*) But he comes on Friday. This is Wednesday. (*She backs away from the door, anxious.*) Nobody comes of a Wednesday. (*She bends down and peers through the letter box.*) If it's my money you're after, there's not a thing in my purse. (*She bites her lip, standing in thought. Loudly.*) Are you from the Assistance? They come any time. I've had them on Monday. They

III

come whenever they choose. It's their right. (*With a smile and growing confidence.*) You're the Assistance, aren't you? (*Her voice rises.*) Are you or aren't you? (*Glass is heard breaking from the bedroom. She runs to the entrance of the bedroom and leaps back, startled; a piece of brick has been thrown through the window.* JOYCE *stares, her mouth trembling. Another piece of brick hurtles through the window, smashing another pane. Screaming.*) It's him. He's breaking in. God Almighty, what shall I do? He'll murder me! (*She stamps on the floor.*) Mary! Mary! (*She runs to the door, opens it and runs out into the passage. Her frantic tones can be heard crying:*) Mrs O'Connor! Mrs O'Connor! (*She runs back into the room; slams the door shut. The lock drops with a crash on to the floor. She picks it up and stares at it and then shrieks with fright.*) It's come off! It's broke! (*She tries to fit the lock back on to the door.*) I've told him so often. I've – told him to – mend it! (*She gives up, breathless. Then she tries to pull the settee out into the room, but gives up and picks up a chair which she pushes against the door and sits on.*) He'll easily fling this aside. Oh, Michael, I'm to be murdered because you're too bone idle to fix a lock. (*There is a prolonged ringing on the doorbell.*) Let me alone! I'm going to report you. I've seen them at the station. They've set a trap. I'm safe in here. We have an extremely strong and reliable Chubb lock on the door. So you're trapped. Ha, ha! The detectives are watching the house. (*The front door is kicked. The chair pushes away and* JOYCE *is flung aside.*) If it's the gun you want, I don't know where he's put it. He's taken it. (*Pauses.*) I may be able to find it. Is that what you want? (*Outside the door a burst of music is heard from a transistor radio. There is knocking. The bell rings. A sudden silence. Laughter. Silence. A splintering of wood.* JOYCE *calls shrilly.*) I've told my hubby. He's seeing someone. You'll laugh on the other side of your face. (*Suddenly giving up all pretence, she bursts into tears.*) Go away. There's a good boy. I don't know what you want. I've no money. Please go away. Please, please, please . . . (*She sobs.*)

COMMENTARY: Joe Orton's *Ruffian on the Stair* is a seriocomic thriller which pushes the conventions of stage terror to their ludicrous limit. Orton takes the stock-in-trade elements of a Hammer Horror movie – the innocent threatened by irrational fear – and gives them a wild farcical twist. As with all his writing, there is a wild, off-the-wall quality, where anything can and usually does happen.

Joyce is utterly serious in this scene. The actor must resist adopting a camp or comic attitude towards the material, which will simply undercut the intention of the speech. Neither Joyce, nor the audience, ever see the intruder. The threat is nothing but stage effects. The actor must create the palpable sense and fear of the invisible menace lurking beyond the front door. The situation Joyce experiences alone in her empty home is an all too familiar one. What the actor can do here to help herself is simply project all those fears and anxieties onto the situation, imagining you see bricks being thrown when none are evident to the audience. Interpret the stage directions to give the monologue its full impact. Joyce registers her fear both vocally and physically. Joyce has an idiom all her own. Notice how her language fluctuates between the banal and the epigrammatic as her mood shifts.

The Rules of the Game
(1919) Luigi Pirandello

Act 1. The smartly furnished drawing-room of Silia Gala's flat in
an Italian town. 1919. Evening.

*Silia Gala (30s) is separated from her husband Leone and has taken a
lover, Guido Venanzi. When Leone comes to call on her now he only
'comes as far as the front door and sends the maid up to ask if I have any
message for him'. She has spent the latter part of the evening 'daydreaming' in her dressing-gown. She is contemplating her life and
freedom, ignoring Guido who has become increasingly irritated by her
self-indulgence. She admits that the only enjoyment she finds as a
woman is to make men miserable. In this scene she explains to Guido
the influence her husband still has over her, and her anger that he no
longer visits her in person.*

SILIA. Don't you see it's the fact of his being alive, his mere
existence that haunts me? It's not his body at all. On the
contrary; it would be much better if I did see him. And it's
just because he knows that, he doesn't let me see him any
more. If he did come in and sit down in that chair over there,
he'd seem like any other man, neither uglier nor better-
looking. I'd see those eyes of his that I never liked – God,
they're horrible. Sharp as needles and vacant at the same
time. I'd hear that voice of his that gets on my nerves. I'd
have something tangible to grapple with – and I'd even get
some satisfaction out of giving him the bother of coming
upstairs for nothing!
[GUIDO. I don't believe it.
SILIA. What don't you believe?
GUIDO. That anything could possibly bother him!
SILIA. Yes, that's the trouble] He's like a ghost, quite
114

detached from life, existing only to haunt other people's lives. I sit for hours on end absolutely crushed by the thought. There he is alone in his own apartment, dressed up as a cook – dressed up as a cook, I ask you! – looking down on everybody from above, watching and understanding every move you make, everything you do, knowing all your thoughts, and making you foresee exactly what you're going to do next – and, of course, when you know what it is, you no longer want to do it! That man has paralysed me! I've only one idea continually gnawing at my brain: how to get rid of him; how to free myself from him.

Translation by Robert Rietty & Noel Cregeen

COMMENTARY: Pirandello's *The Rules of the Game* deals with the nature of role-playing. Suffering and disillusionment, even suicidal tendencies, are hidden behind a mask of dignity and sobriety. Once the mask is pulled away cruel and barbaric impulses stand in wait. Each of the characters in this triangular relationship is multi-faceted and unpredictable. Leone is the representative of pure reason and Silia of pure instinct. The play is a farce of despair.

Silia tries to make Guido believe that it is the very fact of Leone's existence that makes her life a misery. She vividly describes Leone's enigmatically irresistible qualities. Silia's objective may be to make Guido jealous and take action against Leone on her behalf. The actor must decide for herself how much of her denial is a bluff and how much is real torment. There is something unmistakably melodramatic about Silia as she portrays herself as the wronged victim. But there is also a ring of psychological truth in her obsession with her former husband. He still fascinates her to the point of desperation. It is his very existence that 'haunts' her to the point of obsession. Until all trace of him is wiped from her life she will never be free. Earlier in the play Silia espouses her simple ambition, 'I want to be rich . . . my own mistress . . . free!' As it stands her memory of Leone keeps her a prisoner.

The Ruling Class

(1968) Peter Barnes

Act 1, scene 14. The Earl's bedroom in Gurney Manor.

Grace Shelley (20s) is an experienced 'entertainer', singer and cabaret artiste. She is the mistress of Sir Charles Gurney. Jack Gurney, Sir Charles' nephew, who is insane and believes that he is God ('J.C.'), has just inherited the Gurney title and estate, becoming the 14th Earl of Gurney. Sir Charles and the rest of the family want to have Jack declared insane and they can only do this if Jack produces a male heir. However, Jack is convinced that he is already married to Marguerite Gautier, the Lady of the Camellias (the heroine of 'Camille' and 'La Traviata'). Sir Charles persuades Grace to impersonate Marguerite and convince Jack to marry her again. Grace, eager to become Lady Gurney, rises to the challenge. Jack is completely taken in by the deception and delighted with this 'dream made flesh'. The wedding goes ahead and in this monologue Grace anticipates her 'first night' as she gets undressed.

GRACE. I always get first night nerves. Any good performer does. You have to be keyed up to give a good show. I've done it all, from Stanislavski to Strip. Never think I once worked as a stripper, would you? It's true, as God is my witness – no, you weren't there, were you J.C.? Greasy make-up towels, cracked mirrors, rhinestones and beads. What a world. (*Takes off stocking and throws it absently into audience.*) I sang 'This Can't Be Love'. Funny, I did the same act later at the 'Pigalle' for twice the money without removing a stitch. (*Proudly.*) Of course, some women can strip without taking their clothes off. (*She sits on a chair and takes off other stocking.*) Nobody could call me undersexed, but I could never get worked up watching some man strip down to his suspenders and jock strap. Where's the fun? I suppose some people just enjoy the smell of a steak better than the steak itself. (*Throws stocking into audience.*) If my mother could see me now – it's what she always wanted for me – the Big Time. She never forgave Dad for being born in Clapham. Guess she found it hard to settle down to civilian life after being in a touring company of *Chu Chin Chow*. Nobody need worry about me fitting in. (*Walks momentarily into darkness.*) All I have to do is play it cool. (*Reappears into spot, in black nightdress, miming drinking tea with finger cocked up.*) I can cock my little finger with the best.

COMMENTARY: Peter Barnes' gift as a dramatist is to take us inside the world and mind of the English eccentric. He lets the ruling class damn itself through its own strange codes of behaviour. His plays are unsettling and owe little to any type of dramatic convention. Part of their pleasure comes from their seemingly improvisatory freedom. Yet a play like *The Ruling Class*, which seems at first glance an anarchic and chaotic work, resolves itself in complete coherence when performed on stage.

In this monologue Grace takes the audience into her confidence, playfully flirting with them. She has an engaging and easy familiarity as she reminisces about her days as a stripper. It's just another job to her. The actor must capture Grace's lack of inhibition as she undresses, but try not to focus on the act of stripping at the expense of the speech itself. She uses her former experience as a kind of acting warm-up, to help her face the challenges that lie ahead. It's a way of settling nerves and overcoming stage fright. She also knows that being on stage is like appearing naked. So what better way to prepare than by showing a little flesh. For Grace this is just one more role, albeit one with a greater reward than most.

Saint Joan
(1924) Bernard Shaw

Scene 6. A great stone hall in Rouen Castle. 30th May, 1431.

Joan of Arc (18–20) has been brought to trial on charges of heresy and witchcraft. She is abandoned both by the French King whose fortunes she saved from defeat by the English and by the Catholic Church which she fought to defend. She is presented as a naive, innocent victim of male brutality. In Shaw's version Joan's only crime was her 'unwomanly and insufferable presumption'. She becomes a pawn in the intense rivalry between the power of the Church and the State. In this scene she is manipulated into signing a recantation only to find that her reward is to be sentenced to life imprisonment. Joan reveals her full scorn and anger in this speech as she rejects the recantation.

JOAN (*rising in consternation and terrible anger*). Perpetual imprisonment! Am I not then to be set free?

[LAVENDU (*mildly shocked*). Set free, child, after such wickedness as yours! What are you dreaming of?]

Give me that writing. (*She rushes to the table; snatches up the paper; and tears it into fragments.*) Light your fire; do you think I dread it as much as the life of a rat in a hole? My voices were right.

[LAVENDU. Joan! Joan!]

Yes: they told me you were fools (*the word gives great offence*), and that I was not to listen to your fine words nor trust to your charity. You promised me my life; but you lied (*indignant exclamations*). You think that life is nothing but not being stone dead. It is not the bread and water I fear: I can live on bread: when have I asked for more? It is no hardship to drink water if the water be clean. Bread has no sorrow for me, and water no affliction. But to shut me from

118

the light of the sky and the sight of the fields and flowers; to chain my feet so that I can never again ride with the soldiers nor climb the hills; to make me breathe foul damp darkness, and keep from me everything that brings me back to the love of God when your wickedness and foolishness tempt me to hate Him: all this is worse than the furnace in the Bible that was heated seven times. I could do without my warhorse; I could drag about in a skirt; I could let the banners and the trumpet and the knights and the soldiers pass me and leave me behind as they leave the other women, if only I could still hear the wind in the trees, the larks in the sunshine, the young lambs crying through the healthy frost, and the blessed blessed church bells that send my angel voices floating to me on the wind. But without these things I cannot live; and by your wanting to take them away from me, or from any human creature, I know that your counsel is of the devil, and that mine is of God.

COMMENTARY: Shaw's *Saint Joan* explores the meaning and nature of sainthood. In Shaw's opinion, a saint is so threatening to her contemporaries that she has to be destroyed. The central character that Shaw portrays is markedly more brainy than the intuitive version presented by Jean Anouilh in *The Lark* (*see page 73*). She is a fiercely declamatory character whose rhetoric matches that of any man. Her life spirit is so intense that the sudden realization that it will be cut off makes her react. This is clearly one of the most prized female roles in the modern theatre and Joan has been played by the likes of Frances de la Tour, Eileen Atkins, Sybil Thorndike, Joan Plowright and Barbara Jefford.

The problem in performing this speech by Joan is the inclination to let the heart rule the head. If the speech becomes an emotional rant it will snap the thread of the argument. Yet if Joan becomes too rational the speech will sound like cool cynicism. The actor has to balance both sides of the character and find a middle ground. Joan speaks in long complex sentences. These alone can exhaust the unwary performer. The speech requires a lot of breath and ballast. A good caution would be to keep your mind on the message and avoid the emotional traps. Joan's greatest fear is isolation. She is a social animal and verbal interaction is what keeps her alive.

Saved
(1965) Edward Bond

Scene 8. The living room of a house in South London.

Pam (23) is a local 'slag'. She is 'thin, sharp-busted. Heavy nodal hips. Dark hair. Long narrow face. Pale eyes. Small mouth. Looks tall from a distance, but is shorter than she looks.' She lives at home with her parents, Harry and Mary, who have not spoken to one another in years. Pam first picks up Len and then drops him in favour of his mate Fred. Len stays on as a lodger in her parents' house, but Pam finds him increasingly irritating. Pam has Fred's baby, but Fred shows no interest in either mother or son. One day when Pam is in the park pushing the baby in its pram she comes across Fred and his loutish, hooligan friends. In a fit of anger she abandons the baby with Fred. He and his friends, after kicking the pram around, start to stone the baby to death. Fred is arrested and sent to prison. In this scene Pam has heard that Fred is about to be released and is hoping that he will move in with her. She has just washed her hair and comes into the living room. She interrupts her father who is doing his ironing and talking to Len.

PAM. 'Oo's got my *Radio Times?* You 'ad it? (HARRY *doesn't answer. She turns to* LEN.) You?
[LEN (*mumbles*). Not again.]
You speakin' t'me?
[LEN. I'm sick t'death of yer bloody *Radio Times.*]
Someone's 'ad it. (*She rubs her hair vigorously.*) I ain' goin' a get it no more. Not after last week. I'll cancel it. It's the last time I bring it in this 'ouse. I don't see why I ave t'go on paying for it. Yer must think I'm made a money. It's never 'ere when I wan'a see it. Not once. It's always the same. (*She rubs her hair.*) I notice no one else offers t'pay for it. Always Charlie. It's 'appened once too often this time.

[LEN. Every bloody week the same!]

(*To* HARRY.) Sure yer ain't got it?

[HARRY. I bought this shirt over eight years ago.]

That cost me every week. You reckon that up over a year. Yer must think I was born yesterday. (*Pause. She rubs her hair.*) Wasn't 'ere last week. Never 'ere. Got legs. (*She goes to the door and shouts.*) Mum! She 'eard all right. (*She goes back to the couch and sits. She rubs her hair.*) Someone's got it. I shouldn't think the people next door come in an' took it. Everyone 'as the benefit a it 'cept me. It's always the same. I'll know what t'do in future. Two can play at that game. I ain't blinkin' daft. (*She rubs her hair.*) I never begrudge no one borrowin' it, but yer'd think they'd have enough manners t' put it back. (*Pause. She rubs her hair.*) Juss walk all over yer. Well it ain' goin' a 'appen again. They treat you like a door mat. All take and no give. Touch somethin' a their'n an' they go through the bloody ceilin'. It's bin the same ever since –

[LEN. I tol' yer t' keep it in yer room!]

Now yer got a lock things up in yer own 'ouse.

COMMENTARY: Edward Bond's *Saved* is a savage and uncompromising look at England's social underclass. The brutal scene in which Pam's baby is stoned instantly made the play one of the most controversial in modern British drama. The fragmentary writing strains to capture and make articulate the inarticulate sufferings of the poor underclass.

Pam's obsession with the *Radio Times* magazine is just a deflection of a far deeper frustration. In her world ownership of the simplest material object is all. This is also a world in which conversation – polite or otherwise – comes at a premium. If characters speak then they know they exist; know they are important. Pam is also looking for a direction in which to vent her frustration. She's looking for a target and a fight. Notice how she moves about the room in search of the wayward mag, furiously drying her hair as she moves about. She's the sort of woman who would abandon her baby to a gang of thugs but never her *Radio Times*. She speaks in the clamped, guttural accent of South London. All the rudeness of colloquial speech, clipped words and syncopated rhythms come into play in this speech.

The Sea
(1973) Edward Bond

Scene 7. A clifftop on the east coast of England, 1907.

Mrs Louise Rafi (ageing) is a well-off lady living in a coastal town. She shares her house with her companion Mrs Jessica Tilehouse and her young niece Rose. She is a pillar of the local community: a regular churchgoer and the leading light of the local amateur dramatic society. She is domineering and righteous in her Christian beliefs. The town's peaceful calm is shattered when Rose's fiancé, Colin, is drowned at sea in suspicious circumstances. Mrs Rafi organizes a sentimental and dramatic clifftop memorial service for the scattering of Colin's ashes. The service is disrupted first by Mrs Tilehouse and then by the vengeful draper, Hatch, and ends in chaos. Mrs Rafi is left alone on the clifftop with Colin's best friend Willy to muse on the day's events.

MRS RAFI. I'm afraid of getting old. I've always been a forceful woman. I was brought up to be. People expect my class to shout at them. They're disappointed if you don't. It gives them something to gossip about in their bars. When they turn you into an eccentric, it's their form of admiration. Sometimes I think I'm like a lighthouse in their world. I give them a sense of order and security. My glares mark out a channel to the safe harbour. I'm so tired of them. I'm tired of being a sideshow in their little world. Nothing else was open to me. If I were a Catholic – (*She looks round.*) – it's all right, the vicar's gone – I'd have been an Abbess. I'd have terrified the nuns. They'd have loved it. Like living next door to the devil. But the grand old faith didn't allow me even that consolation. Of course I have my theatricals – (*She looks round as before.*) – yes, the ladies have gone – none of them can act, you know. Oh no. I'm surrounded by mediocrities.

124

A flaming torch and no path to shine on . . . I'll grow old and shout at them from a wheelchair. That's what they're waiting for. They get their own back for all the years I bullied them. They wheel you where they like. 'Take me there.' 'You went there yesterday. We want to go the other way.' 'Take me down to the beach. I want to see the sea.' 'You don't want to see the sea. You saw the sea yesterday. The wind's bad for your head. If you misbehave and catch cold we'll shut you up in bed. You'll stay there for good this time.' Subtle. Jessica would probably stick matchsticks under my nails. I'll see she's pensioned off. She is one of those ladies who are meant to die alone in a small room. You give up shouting. You close your eyes and the tears dribble down your ugly old face and you can't even wipe it clean – they won't give you your hanky. 'Don't let her have it. She gets into a tizzy and tears it to shreds.' There you are: old, ugly, whimpering, dirty, pushed about on wheels and threatened. I can't love them. How could I? But that's a terrible state in which to move towards the end of your life: to have no love. Has anything been worthwhile? No. I've thrown my life away. (*She sees someone offstage.*) Come along. They've gone.

COMMENTARY: One never thinks of the uncompromising plays of Edward Bond as being filled with comic moments. Yet they do come at odd times in plays like *The Sea*. Bond's brand of comedy, like that of Bernard Shaw, reveals itself in the self-reverential ways that characters portray themselves. Bond wants us to be drawn to his characters but also remain distanced from them. It is their contrariness that keeps us off balance. Actresses like Coral Browne and Judi Dench have been superb at making this monolith of a woman seem touched by human vanity and even silliness.

In this speech Mrs Rafi shares an unguarded moment of candour with us and the character on stage. The speech is distinguished by its Shavian and Brechtian size; Mrs Rafi is self-consciously aware that she is 'forceful' and 'eccentric', almost a freak of human nature; one of life's stage manageresses. In the second half of the speech she seems genuinely touched with emotion, and this is hinted at at the top of the monologue. This is an elderly woman who is aging. So that lamentable process must be taken on board by the actress. But notice that there is nothing sentimental or melodramatic about the way Mrs Rafi speaks. She's a tough old thing who does not so much speak as make pronouncements.

Sexual Perversity in Chicago
(1974) David Mamet

One act. Joan and Deb's apartment. Chicago. The evening.

Joan Webber (late 20s) is single and teaches in a Nursery School. She is smart and sociable. She shares an apartment with Deb who has started dating Danny. Joan has been chatted up by the straight-talking Bernie in a singles bar, but she has been less than enthusiastic about him. Here the two women are spending a night in.

JOAN. I don't know, I don't know. I don't know, I don't know. I don't know.
(*Pause.*)
[DEBORAH. You don't know what?]
I don't know anything, Deborah, I swear to God, the older I get the less I know. (*Pause.*) It's a puzzle. Our efforts at coming to grips with ourselves . . . in an attempt to become 'more human' (which, in itself, is an interesting concept). It has to do with an increased ability to recognize *clues* . . . and the control of energy in the form of *lust* . . . and *desire* (and also in the form of hope) . . . But a *finite* puzzle. Whose true solution lies, perhaps, in transcending the rules themselves . . . (*Pause.*) . . . and pounding of the fucking pieces into places where they DO NOT FIT AT ALL. (*Pause.*) Those of us who have seen the hands of the Master Magician move a bit too slowly do have a rough time from time to time. (*Pause.*) Some things persist. (*Pause.*) 'Loss' is always possible.

COMMENTARY: *Sexual Perversity in Chicago* captures in comic vignettes the dating and mating habits of urban life. The play chronicles the relationships and sexual encounters of two young men and two young women over the course of a summer. Mamet excels at creating carefully observed, highly idiomatic contemporary dialogue.

Joan's contorted speech pattern is full of denials and ellipses; gaps where thoughts should be. She really doesn't know what to say and what she does say is full of evasion. Notice how she is meant to phrase certain words in italics and full capital letters. Throughout, the speech is pitched into different rhythms and the task for the performer is to find a comfortable way of working with the character's loopy phrases like 'a rough time from time to time'. The speech is full of comic potential that comes from straining to communicate but, in the end, saying nothing.

Nursery School.

Joan is lecturing two toddlers.

JOAN. What are you doing? Where are you going? What are you doing? You stay right there. Now. What were the two of you doing? I'm just asking a simple question. There's nothing to be ashamed of. (*Pause.*) I can wait. (*Pause.*) Were you playing 'Doctor'? (*Pause.*) 'Doctor.' Don't play dumb with me, just answer the question. (You know, that attitude is going to get you in a lot of trouble someday.) Were you playing with each other's genitals? Each other's . . . 'pee-pees'? . . . whatever you call them at home, that's what I'm asking (and don't play dumb, because I saw what you were doing, so just own up to it.) (*Pause.*) All right . . . no. No, stop that, there's no reason for tears . . . it's perfectly . . . natural. But . . . there's a time and a place for everything. Now . . . no it's all right. Come on. Come on, we're all going in the other room, and we're going to wash our hands. And then Miss Webber is going to call our parents.

COMMENTARY: Joan is on the verge of being out of control. One can imagine her with toddlers going every which way. The speech requires lots of physical contortions and the kind of over-explicit, strained communication that comes from talking to children. The performer has to decide for herself how big a gang of kids she is shepherding, and create a sense of them for the audience. The subject of the speech is sex. Joan has to be an authority figure but might show embarrassment. She certainly becomes upset when her charges begin to cry. Joan has enough trouble taking care of herself and her own emotional life. The complex world of child psychology is just the sort of minefield she would have to cross gingerly.

Spring Awakening
(1892) Frank Wedekind

Act 2, scene 7. A path near the river in a provincial German town.
1892.

Ilse (14) is a free-spirited girl who has dropped out from school and run away to live amongst the artists (known as the 'Phallustics' who have adopted the names of famous artists) and the demi-monde in town. In this scene, after a four day binge, she is on her way home to her mother when she encounters the deeply depressed Moritz, one of her childhood friends. She gives him a detailed account of her joyous, bohemian existence as an artists' model. She has on her dancing shoes and is in a celebratory mood.

ILSE. You've only got to look at you, Moritz! I don't know what a hangover is! Last carnival I didn't go to bed or get out of my clothes for three days and nights! From Fancy Dress Balls to the cafés, lunch on the lake, cellar revues in the evenings, nights back to the Fancy Dress Balls. Lena was with me and that fat Viola. Heinrich found me on the third night.
[MORITZ. Was he looking for you?]
He tripped over my arm. I was lying unconscious on the street in the snow. Afterwards I went back to his place. I couldn't get away for two weeks – that was a terrible time! Every morning I had to pose in his Persian dressing gown, and every evening walk round his rooms in a black page-boy tunic. White lace, cuffs, collar and knees. He photographed me in a different way every day – once as Ariadne on the arm of the sofa, once as Leda, once as Ganymede, and once on all fours as a female Nobodycanesor. He was always squirming on about murder, shooting, suicide, drugs and fumes. He

brought a pistol in bed every morning, loaded it with shot, and pushed it into my breast: one twitch and I press. O, he would have pressed, Moritz, he would have pressed. Then he put the thing in his mouth like a pea-shooter. It's supposed to be good for the self-preservation instinct. Ugh – the bullet would have gone through my spine!

[MORITZ. Is Heinrich still alive?

ILSE. How should I know?] There was a big mirror in the ceiling over the bed. The little room looked as tall as a tower, as bright as an opera house. You saw yourself hanging down alive from the sky. I had terrible dreams. God, O God, if only the day would come. Good night, Ilse. When you're asleep you're so beautiful I could murder you.

[MORITZ. Is this Heinrich still alive?

ILSE. No, please God.] One day he was fetching absinthe and I threw my coat on and slipped out in the street. The carnival was over. The police picked me up. What was I doing in men's clothes? They took me to the station. Then Nohl, Karl, Paganini, Schiller and El Greco, all the Phallustics, came and stood bail for me. They carried me home in a posh cab. Since then I've stuck to the crowd. Karl's an ape, Nohl's a pig, Berlioz's a goat, Dostoyevsky's a hyena, El Greco's a bear – but I love them, all of them together, and I wouldn't trust anyone else even if the world was full of saints and millionaires.

Translation by Edward Bond

COMMENTARY: Wedekind's *Spring Awakening* focuses on a group of adolescents as they awaken to their sexuality and come into inevitable conflict with their repressive parents and teachers. Moritz and his friends are sympathetically presented with all their fears, delights and neuroses fully revealed. Almost like a painting, the play uses bold, colourful images to create a canvas of dreamlike urges and fantasies that touch the audience with their explicit honesty. Today, one hundred years after its first notorious performance, it still manages to provoke audiences with its frank portrayal of sexuality.

Ilse gives the naive Moritz a vivid picture of a forbidden and decadent lifestyle. The actor must decide how much of this is made up. Each image should pulsate with titillation. Ilse has been part of a graphic, dizzying world in which intoxication is a key component. The story and incidents she relates must mesmerise the listener. Nothing about her delivery is static or matter-of-fact. She is a true bohemian with a lust for life and very much at the centre of her tale. She is like the Blue Angel: part innocent and part demonic woman. The performer has to approach this speech without embarrassment. In fact, the purpose of the speech should be to provoke a response. This is a character who thrives on carnival and excess. Life to her is a thrill.

A Streetcar Named Desire
(1947) Tennessee Williams

Scene 10. The bedroom of an apartment building in a street in New Orleans which is named Elysian Fields.

Blanche DuBois (30) has come to New Orleans to stay with her younger sister Stella and her husband Stanley. 'Her delicate beauty must avoid a strong light.' She has cultivated the delicate manners and charm of a Southern lady, but this artful façade merely hides a neurotic and broken personality. Through the course of the play it becomes apparent that Blanche's stories are merely a tissue of lies masking her promiscuous and alcoholic lifestyle. Stanley realizes that she has squandered the family inheritance and sees through her feigned gentility. He has introduced her to one of his workmates, Mitch and they find themselves attracted to one another. Blanche's hopes of marriage are shattered when Stanley tells Mitch the truth about her. Earlier that evening Mitch has bluntly rejected Blanche and since then she has been drinking steadily. In this scene, Stanley has just returned from the hospital where Stella is waiting to give birth. Blanche has been regaling the sceptical Stanley with tales of a Texas millionaire who has telegrammed to summon her to him.

BLANCHE. When I think of how divine it is going to be to have such a thing as privacy once more – I could weep with joy!
[STANLEY. This millionaire from Dallas is not going to interfere with your privacy any?]
It won't be the sort of thing you have in mind. This man is a gentleman and he respects me. (*Improvising feverishly.*) What he wants is my companionship. Having great wealth sometimes makes people lonely! A cultivated woman, a woman of intelligence and breeding, can enrich a man's life – immeasurably! I have those things to offer, and this doesn't

take them away. Physical beauty is passing. A transitory possession. But beauty of the mind and richness of the spirit and tenderness of the heart – and I have all those things – aren't taken away, but grow! Increase with the years! How strange that I should be called a destitute woman! When I have all of these treasures locked in my heart. (*A choked sob comes from her.*) I think of myself as a very, very rich woman! But I have been foolish – casting my pearls before swine!

[STANLEY. Swine, huh?]

Yes, swine! And I'm thinking not only of you but of your friend, Mr Mitchell. He came to see me tonight. He dared to come here in his work-clothes! And to repeat slander to me, vicious stories that he had gotten from you! I gave him his walking papers . . .

[STANLEY. You did, huh?]

But then he came back. He returned with a box of roses to beg my forgiveness. But some things are not forgivable. Deliberate cruelty is not forgivable. It is the one unforgivable thing in my opinion and it is the one thing of which I have never, never been guilty. And so I told him, I said to him, 'Thank you,' but it was foolish of me to think that we could ever adapt ourselves to each other. Our ways of life are too different. Our attitudes and backgrounds are incompatible. We have to be realistic about such things. So farewell, my friend! And let there be no hard feelings . . .

COMMENTARY: Blanche DuBois, in a *Streetcar Named Desire*, is undoubedly the greatest female role in modern American drama. Actresses as varied as Jessica Tandy, Vivien Leigh and Jessica Lange have played this doomed, fragile character in quite different yet exquisite ways. Like all of Tennessee Williams' best heroines, Blanche exists in a self-absorbed world of delusions. Beauty, grandeur and youth are masks that she slips on as protective devices to shield her from the brutality of savages like Stanley Kowalski.

Blanche's best defence when she speaks is the protesting exclamation. She hurls her first sentence in Stanley's face and each subsequent one has the same shield-like purpose. She is easily provoked and aroused. Stanley stalks Blanche. She is constantly eluding his trap. Here she keeps him at bay with a breathless series of sentences. She literally makes up her story about the Texan as she goes along, always sensing that Stanley knows she is lying. Her effort always is to stay one step ahead of him, just beyond his clutches. So one untruth after another must be fabricated as a further defence. Notice that Stanley's retorts are like short, sharp pounces. He is after Blanche and she knows it. Blanche is scared of him; maybe she keeps backing away with her words. Like a virgin before a barbarian, she invokes purity and high-mindedness as her defence. She also bids adieu to her Texan hero as, like a mirage, he evaporates in the midst of Stanley's onslaught. His disappearance is also a good image for Blanche's running out of steam. At this point in the play, as well, Blanche is becoming more erratic and confused. Illusion and reality are very much the same thing to her.

Summer and Smoke
(1948) Tennessee Williams

Scene 11. The office of Dr John Buchanan, Jr. Five o'clock on a winter evening in a year shortly before the First World War.

Alma Winemiller is the daughter of a minister and his unstable wife. She 'had an adult quality as a child and now in her middle twenties, there is something prematurely spinsterish about her. . . . People her own age regard her as quaintly and humorously affected.' After several years absence, Dr John Buchanan, Jr. returns to town and takes over his father's practice. He is a wild, charming and dissipated character; the complete opposite of Alma who tries to persuade him to be more responsible. During the summer John invites Alma to Moon Lake Casino, suggesting that they rent a private room. Her reaction is to flee. Several months later Alma comes to John's office to offer herself to him. But he has seen the error of his former ways in favour of the spiritual commitment that she had advocated. He has just rejected Alma's proposition and this is her response.

ALMA. Oh, I suppose I am sick, one of those weak and divided people who slip like shadows among you solid strong ones. But sometimes, out of necessity, we shadowy people take on a strength of our own. I have that now. You needn't try to deceive me.
[JOHN. I wasn't.]
You needn't try to comfort me. I haven't come here on any but equal terms. You said, let's talk truthfully, even shamelessly, then! It's no longer a secret that I love you. It never was. I loved you as long ago as the time I asked you to read the stone angel's name with your fingers. Yes, I remember the long afternoons of our childhood, when I had to stay indoors to practise my music – and heard your
136

playmates calling you, 'Johnny, Johnny!' How it went through me, just to hear your name called! And how I – rushed to the window to watch you jump the porch railing! I stood at a distance, halfway down the block, only to keep in sight of your torn red sweater, racing about the vacant lot you played in. Yes, it had begun that early, this affliction of love, and has never let go of me since, but kept on growing. I've lived next door to you all the days of my life, a weak and divided person who stood in adoring awe of your singleness, of your strength. And that is my story! Now I wish *you* would tell *me* – why didn't it happen beween us? Why did I fail? Why did you come almost close enough – and no closer?

COMMENTARY: In *Summer and Smoke* Tennessee Williams generates conflict as prim rectitude clashes with passionate desire. Most of Williams' modern gothic tragedies are set between these two competing viewpoints. His plays are inhabited by a type of character who, in his own words in this play, is 'faded and frightened and difficult and odd and lonely.' All these traits must emerge in the acting.

Alma teaches the performer an essential fact about acting a Williams character: they emerge at their strongest and most powerful when they are at their weakest. Alma finds strength in defeat. She actually seems like a towering character amidst her pathetic loneliness. When a Williams character portrays her isolation in speeches like this (see also Blanche in *A Streetcar Named Desire*, page 133 and Amanda in *The Glass Menagerie*, page 41) they take on luminescent stature. The childhood self that Alma remembers must seem to us grand and long-suffering. She is the quintessential outsider who has become expert at dramatising her plight. The audience is drawn to her precisely because her sorrow is so exquisitely portrayed in both word and image. Williams offers the actor a useful performance note: 'In Alma's voice and manner there is a delicacy and elegance, a kind of "airiness", which is really natural to her as it is, in a less marked degree, to many Southern girls. Her gestures and mannerisms are a bit exaggerated, but in a graceful way. It is understandable that she might be accused of "putting on airs" and of being "affected" by the other young people of the town. She seems to belong to a more elegant age, such as the eighteenth century in France. Out of nervousness and self-consciousness she has a habit of prefacing and concluding her remarks with a little breathless laugh . . . the characterization must never be stressed to the point of making her at all ludicrous in a less than sympathetic way.'

Ubu Rex
(1896) Alfred Jarry

Act 5, scene 1. Night.

Ma Ubu (30s–40s) is married to Pa Ubu, 'a fat oaf'. She has urged him (Lady Macbeth-like) to kill the Polish King. Pa Ubu recruits Captain Bordure to be his crony, but when Ubu double crosses him Bordure flees to Russia and allies himself with the Tsar against the Ubus. In Warsaw Ma and Pa Ubu rule with ruthless tyranny, imposing outrageous taxes to raise money ('phynances') and authorizing the execution of all the nobles with their debraining machine. In all this they are supported by their ruthless henchmen, the Palcontents. The always greedy Ma Ubu even starts embezzling money from Pa Ubu. Prince Boggerlas, the son of the murdered King of Poland, leads a successful rebellion against the Ubus who are forced to flee. As they are pursued by the Polish army they encounter the advancing Russian army. In this scene Ma Ubu recounts the details of her flight.

MA UBU. Shelter at last! I'm alone here, which is fine as far as I'm concerned, but what a dreadful journey: crossing the whole of Poland in four days! Every possible misfortune struck me at the same moment. As soon as that great, fat oaf had clattered off on his nag I crept into the crypt to grab the treasure, but then everything went wrong. I just escaped being stoned to death by Boggerlas and his madmen. I lost my gallant Palcontent Gyron who was so enamoured of my charms that he swooned with delight every time he saw me and even, I've been told, every time he didn't see me – and there can be no higher love than that. Poor boy, he would have let himself be cut in half for my sake, and the proof is that Boggerlas cut him in quarters. Biff, bam, boom! Ooh, I thought it was all up with me. Then I fled for my life with the bloodthirsty mob hard on my heels. I managed to get out of the palace and reach the Vistula, but all the bridges were guarded. I swam across the river, hoping to shake off my pursuers. The entire nobility rallied and joined in the chase. I nearly breathed my last a thousand times, half smothered by the surrounding Poles all screaming for my blood. Finally, I escaped their clutches, and after four days of trudging through the snows of what was once my kingdom have at last reached refuge here. I've had nothing to eat or drink these past four days, and Boggerlas breathing down my neck the whole time. Now here I am, safe at last. Ah! I'm dead with exhaustion and hunger. But I'd give a lot to know what became of my big fat buffoon, I mean to say my esteemed spouse. Lord, how I've skinned him, and relieved him of his rix-dollars! I've certainly rolled him plenty! And his phynance charger that was dying of hunger – it didn't get oats to munch very often, poor beast! It was fun while it lasted, but alas, I had to leave my treasure behind in Warsaw, where it's up for grabs.

Translation by Cyril Connolly and Simon Watson Taylor

COMMENTARY: Alfred Jarry's *Ubu* plays are outrageous satires on cruelty, power and dictatorship. Jarry created a unique theatrical style which combined elements of the farce and puppet play. Pere Ubu is a gross monster, part Macbeth and part Henry VIII, who tortures and kills at the slightest whim. He is the spirit of annihilation who coddles with one hand and crushes with the other. Ma Ubu, a combination of Lady Macbeth and Elena Ceausescu, uses her husband to satisfy her own lust for power and fortune. Both he and she, a kind of Punch and Judy double act, are also the dark spirits of oppression that roam throughout modern history.

Ma Ubu has travelled far and wide. She is exhausted and yet full of stories that must be urgently told through her weariness. The carnage she describes has a cartoon-like quality helped along by all the nonsense words invented by Jarry and then newly invented in this translation. A living actor, however, must find some degree of reality in so ridiculous a creation. Recent history in the former states of 'Eastern' Europe and the Balkan countries give Ma Ubu's farcical tales a grim and disturbing reality. A performer might try to fuse fact and fiction together in order to drive the speech with acrid hilarity.

A View from the Bridge
(1955) Arthur Miller

Act 2. The living room-dining room of Eddie Carbone's apartment. It is a worker's flat, clean, sparse, homely.

Catherine (17) is an orphan and lives with her uncle, Eddie Carbone and his wife, Beatrice. He treats her like a daughter and lavishes protective love on her. Two of his wife's Sicilian cousins illegally enter the country and Catherine falls in love with one of them, Rodolpho. But Eddie becomes jealous and suspicious of Rodolpho, arguing that he only wants to marry Catherine to become an American citizen. In this scene, Rodolpho and Catherine, alone together in the house for the first time, are talking about their marriage plans and Eddie.

CATHERINE. It's only that I – He was good to me, Rodolpho. You don't know him; he was always the sweetest guy to me. Good. He razzes me all the time but don't mean it. I know. I would – just feel ashamed if I made him sad. 'Cause I always dreamt that when I got married he would be happy at the wedding, and laughin' – and now he's mad all the time and nasty – (*She is weeping.*) Tell him you'd live in Italy – just tell him, and maybe he would start to trust you a little, see? Because I want him to be happy; I mean – I like him, Rodolpho – and I can't stand it!
[RODOLPHO. Oh, Catherine – oh, little girl.]
I love you, Rodolpho, I love you.
[RODOLPHO. Then why are you afraid? That he'll spank you?]
Don't, don't laugh at me! I've been here all my life. . . . Every day I saw him when he left in the morning and when he came home at night. You think it's so easy to turn around and say to a man he's nothin' to you no more?

[RODOLPHO. I know, but –]

You don't know; nobody knows! I'm not a baby, I know a lot more than people think I know. Beatrice says to be a woman, but –

[RODOLPHO. Yes.]

Then why don't she be a woman? If I was a wife I would make a man happy instead of goin' at him all the time. I can tell a block away when he's blue in his mind and just wants to talk to somebody quiet and nice. . . . I can tell when he's hungry or wants a beer before he even says anything. I know when his feet hurt him, I mean I *know* him and now I'm supposed to turn around and make a stranger of him? I don't know why I have to do that, I mean. . . . Hold me. . . . Teach me. (*She is weeping.*) I don't know anything, teach me, Rodolpho, hold me.

COMMENTARY: Miller's *A View from the Bridge*, set in the waterfront district of Brooklyn during the 1950s, is a modern tragedy about repressed desires, loyalty, honour and betrayal. But rather than focus on noble heroes and heroines, Miller finds nobility in the lives of a lowly longshoreman and his tightly knit family. Each of the relatively inarticulate characters is forced to disclose raw passions that both surprise and disturb them when spoken aloud.

Catherine is torn between two men in this speech. Rodolpho is the man she loves but through him she projects an even greater love and attachment to Eddie. Eddie has been like a father to her but is also something like a secret lover. Part of the confusion Catherine suffers here (notice how fragmentary the speech is) comes from the fact that she is involved in two separate triangular relationships: Catherine-Rodolpho-Eddie and Catherine-Rodolpho-Beatrice. Yet she never quite comprehends the implications of her emotional entanglements. The speech is such a challenge to act because the character is torn between two opposing poles, both offering her love and comfort. Throughout the drama Catherine is an innocent without any sense of deceit or corruption. The future tragedy in the play must be sensed in moments like this.

Who's Afraid of Virginia Woolf?
(1962) Edward Albee

Act 1, 'Fun and Games'. The living room of a house on the campus of a small New England college.

Martha is 'a large, boisterous woman, 52, looking somewhat younger. Ample, but not fleshy.' She has been married to George, six years her junior, for over twenty years. He teaches history at the college run by Martha's father. They have invited Nick and Honey, a new young faculty couple, over for drinks. By the time their guests arrive they have already had several drinks and are both in a combative mood. Martha dresses to look 'most voluptuous'. Earlier in the scene Martha had been taunting George and mildly flirting with Nick, she is now alone with Nick and Honey.

MARTHA. [Him? Oh, sure.] George and I had this boxing match . . . Oh, Lord, twenty years ago . . . a couple of years after we were married.
[NICK. A boxing match? The two of you?
HONEY. Really?]
Yup . . . the two of us really.
[HONEY (*with a little shivery giggle of anticipation*). I can't imagine it.]
Well, like I say, it was twenty years ago, and it wasn't in a ring, or anything like that, you know what I mean. It was wartime, and Daddy was on this physical fitness kick . . . Daddy's always admired physical fitness . . . says a man is only part brain . . . he has a body too, and it's his responsibility to keep both of them up . . . you know?
[NICK. Unh-hunh.]
Says the brain can't work unless the body's working, too.
[NICK. Well, that's not exactly so . . .]

Well, maybe that *isn't* what he says . . . something like it. *But* . . . it was wartime, and Daddy got the idea all the men should learn how to box . . . self-defense. I suppose the idea was if the Germans landed on the coast, or something, the whole faculty'd go out and punch 'em to death. . . . I don't know.

[NICK. It was probably more the principle of the thing.]

No kidding. Anyway, so Daddy had a couple of us over one Sunday and we went out in the back, and Daddy put on the gloves himself. Daddy's a strong man. . . . Well, *you* know.

[NICK. Yes . . . yes.]

And he asked George to box with him. Aaaaannnnd . . . George didn't *want* to . . . probably something about not wanting to bloody-up his meal ticket. . . .

[NICK. Unh-hunh.]

. . . Anyway, George said he didn't want to, and Daddy was saying, 'Come on, young man . . . what sort of son-in-law *are* you?' . . . and stuff like that.

[NICK. Yeah.]

So, while this was going on . . . I don't know why I *did* it . . . I got into a pair of gloves myself . . . you know, I didn't lace 'em up, or anything . . . and I snuck up behind George, just kidding, and I yelled 'Hey George!' and at the same time I let go sort of a roundhouse right . . . just kidding, you know?

[NICK. Unh-hunh.]

. . . and George wheeled around real quick, and he caught it right in the jaw . . . POW! (NICK *laughs.*) I hadn't meant it honestly. Anyway . . . POW! Right in the jaw . . . and he was off balance . . . he must have been . . . and he stumbled back a few steps, and then, CRASH, he landed . . . flat . . in a huckleberry bush! (NICK *laughs.* HONEY *goes tsk, tsk, tsk, tsk, and shakes her head.*) It was awful, really. It was funny, but it was awful. (*She thinks, gives a muffled laugh in rueful contemplation of the incident.*) I think it's coloured our whole life. Really I do! It's an excuse, anyway. (GEORGE *enters now, his hands behind his back. No one sees him.*) It's what he uses for being bogged down, anyway . . . why he hasn't *gone* anywhere. And it was an *accident* . . . a real, goddamn accident!

COMMENTARY: Albee's *Who's Afraid of Virginia Woolf?* is a powerful drama of confrontation. George and Martha are locked in a physically intense and emotionally violent love-hate relationship. Alcohol fuels their caustic passions. Their innocent guests also become enmeshed in the psychological and pugilistic mind-games. As the evening wears on the realities of the present and truth of the past are revealed and confronted; one by one dreams and delusions are shattered and destroyed.

Martha uses her guests to get at George. The enmity between husband and wife is intense and finds an outlet in theatrical games full of hidden barbs. A cocktail party and polite conversations, for instance, are merely charades. George and Martha are expert at masking their real motives and personalities behind a barrier of civility. The story Martha tells, though it might seem light and funny, reveals the sexual battle that defines her marriage to George. Notice how much Martha relishes performing her story. Martha is more a 'man' than her husband, more her father's son than daughter. As the play goes on to reveal, Martha is also an emasculating man-eater. The actor must play both sides of the character: her aggressiveness and also her seductiveness. She is extremely vengeful and wilful. An only child she is a good deal older than her husband and has stayed in the world where she grew up. She is neurotic and finds in drink a temporary escape that also hides lots of terror. Any performance must capture the character's essential instability.

Play Sources

Absent Friends by Alan Ayckbourn in *Three Plays* (Penguin)
After the Fall by Arthur Miller in *Miller Plays: Two* (Methuen)
Antigone by Jean Anouilh in *Anouilh: Five Plays* (Methuen)
The Balcony by Jean Genet (Faber)
The Bald Prima Donna by Eugène Ionesco in *Plays: Volume 1* (John Calder)
Blithe Spirit by Noël Coward in *Coward Plays: Four* (Methuen)
Blues for Mister Charlie by James Baldwin (Samuel French)
Cat on a Hot Tin Roof by Tennessee Williams (Penguin)
Cloud Nine by Caryl Churchill in *Churchill Plays: One* (Methuen)
The Cocktail Party by T. S. Eliot (Faber)
A Day in the Death of Joe Egg by Peter Nichols in *Nichols Plays: One* (Methuen)
East by Steven Berkoff (Faber)
Faith Healer by Brian Friel in *Selected Plays* (Faber)
The Glass Menagerie by Tennessee Williams (Penguin)
The Good Person of Sichuan by Bertolt Brecht (Methuen)
Happy Days by Samuel Beckett (Faber)
Hello and Goodbye by Athol Fugard in *Selected Plays* (Oxford University Press)
The House of Blue Leaves by John Guare (Samuel French & Methuen)
Huis Clos [No Exit/In Camera] by Jean-Paul Sartre in *In Camera and Other Plays* (Penguin)
Icarus's Mother by Sam Shepard (Faber)
The Iceman Cometh by Eugene O'Neill (Nick Hern Books)
Jumpers by Tom Stoppard (Faber)
La Turista by Sam Shepard in *Seven Plays* (Faber)
The Lark by Jean Anouilh in *Five Plays* (Methuen)
Long Day's Journey into Night by Eugene O'Neill (Nick Hern Books)

Acknowledgements

The editors and publishers gratefully acknowledge permission to reproduce copyright material in this book:

Edward Albee: from *Who's Afraid of Virginia Woolf?* Copyright © 1962 by Edward Albee. Reprinted by permission of Jonathan Cape. Jean Anouilh: from *Antigone*, trans. Barbara Bray. Copyright © 1987 by Jean Anouilh and Barbara Bray. From *The Lark*, trans. Christopher Fry. Copyright © 1955 by Jean Anouilh and Christopher Fry. Both reprinted by permission of Methuen London. Alan Ayckbourn: from *Absent Friends*. Copyright © 1977 by Alan Ayckbourn. First published by Chatto and Windus in *Three Plays* (1977). Reprinted by permission of Chatto and Windus and Grove Press, Inc. James Baldwin: from *Blues for Mister Charlie*. Copyright © 1964 by James Baldwin. Reprinted by permission of Bantam Doubleday Dell Publishing Group, Inc. Peter Barnes: from *The Ruling Class*. Copyright © 1969, 1989 by Peter Barnes. Reprinted by permission of Methuen London. Samuel Beckett: from *Happy Days*. Copyright © 1959, 1961 by Samuel Beckett. Reprinted by permission of Faber and Faber Ltd and Grove Press. Steven Berkoff: from *East*. Copyright © 1977, 1978 by Steven Berkoff. Reprinted by permission of Faber and Faber Ltd. Edward Bond: from *Saved*. Copyright © 1965, 1977 by Edward Bond. First published in 1966 by Methuen & Co. From *The Sea*. Copyright © 1973, 1978 by Edward Bond. First published in 1973 by Eyre Methuen Ltd. All reprinted by permission of Methuen London. Bertolt Brecht: from *The Good Person of Sichuan*, trans. Michael Hofmann. Translation copyright © 1989 by Stefan S. Brecht. Original work entitled *Der gute Mensch von Setzuan*. Copyright © 1955 by Suhrkamp Verlag, Berlin. Reprinted by permission of Methuen London. Caryl Churchill: from *Cloud Nine*. Copyright © 1979 by Caryl Churchill and Andy Roberts. Reprinted by permission of Methuen London. Albert Camus: from *The Misunderstanding*, trans. Stuart Gilbert. Original work copyright © 1944 Libraire Gallimard. Reprinted by permission of Hamish Hamilton Ltd, Random House Inc. and Editions

acknowledgements. If any errors have occurred, they will be corrected in subsequent editions, provided notification is sent to the publisher.